Leadership INSIGHT:

12 Powerful Secrets Every GREAT Team Leader MUST Know!

Phillip E. Rosner, Ph.D.

HRD USA

HRD PUBLISHING
HUMAN RESOURCE DEVELOPMENT, INC.
MARIETTA, GA

ISBN: 978-0-9973050-0-5

DEDICATION

To my wife, Peri, who comes from my home planet, who I will
love all the rest of my life and who is the only person I have ever
wanted to grow old with …
To my family, Seth, Chelsea, Jacob and Alicia, who form the fabric
of love that has always surrounded me …
To my teachers, who nurtured in me a love of learning and made
my professional life possible …
To my clients, who for some magical reason pay me to do the
work I love so much …
and
To all the people whose friendship I have been blessed to have as I
wander through life …

I humbly dedicate this book.

Table of Contents

Acknowledgements...vii

Introduction 1

My Personal Preface:...5

How to Read This Book:.. 19

Chapter ONE   -   Let's Start at the Beginning 21

Chapter TWO -   What is a leader?............................. 31

Chapter THREE - SEE What is happening 45

    Secret 1. THE Law of Psychology (The Law of Reinforcement).....49

    Secret 2. Content versus Process (Who is doing what, to whom?")..59

    Secret 3. Multiple Levels of Behavior 67

Chapter FOUR - Understanding People 79

Secret 4. Thoughts versus feelings 81

Secret 5. Internal vs. External Locus of Control (LOC) 87

Chapter FIVE - Understanding Teams 95

Secret 6. Teams Desire Democratic Values 97

Secret 7. An Innate Sense of Right and Wrong 103

Chapter SIX - GUIDING Your Team 109

Secret 8. Facilitation: A Word with TWO Meanings 113

Secret 9. Critical Incidents (CI) 119

Secret 10. Intervention Theory 125

Secret 11. Modeling Behavior 137

Secret 12. Decision-Making: Cooperation vs. Collaboration 143

Chapter SEVEN - Now you SEE it – Before you didn't! 153

Chapter EIGHT - Afterthoughts 159

Acknowledgements

Thanks to those kind souls who informally edited the initial drafts of this book and to whom I cannot express enough gratitude: Robert W, Levin, Steve Ehrlich and Al Hutfles.

Thanks to my editor, Christine Adamec, MBA, for her assistance. She is available at www.christineadamec.com

Introduction

Leadership is a critical skill that carries major consequences in today's business world. The team leader's biggest headaches are deciding what problems need to be fixed and then determining how to fix them. Applying resources and effort to the WRONG problem can result in loss of market share, competitive edge, and profitability. Selecting the correct problem to fix requires that the leader sees and understands the complexities of how his work group is operating and also knows how to make the needed changes.

Leadership INSIGHT has been designed to "open your eyes" and:

1. Allow you to see what is happening in your team situation
2. Understand what it means and
3. Select not only the correct problem to work on, but also the correct way to intervene.

After decades of working with senior executives in companies ranging from Fortune 100s to start-ups, Dr. Rosner, an organizational psychologist and a team leadership expert, reveals the twelve most significant concepts in seeing, understanding, and changing people's behavior in the workplace. This "how to" book emphasizes discovering, understanding, and building your practical skills so that they can be used immediately to improve your leadership ability.

This book allows you to see what has always been happening in your work group. Dr. Rosner explains why you never saw it before and shows you how to practice these new skills until you become proficient in their use.

Al H., president of a long-time corporate client of Dr. Rosner, says, "I read the book over the weekend. When I held my next senior executive team meeting on Monday, I was almost overwhelmed by all the things I could see and understand. After a while, I realized that the meeting was pretty typical for us, but those 'typical' behaviors suddenly had new meaning for me. What an eye-opening experience."

Dr. Rosner personally promises that, if you read and apply these concepts, you will be rewarded with:

- A clearer picture of your team and how it works
- A better understanding of why your team does what it does
- A systematic approach to leading more effectively to bring about desired changes
- Greater peace of mind and confidence in your leadership skills

Why wait another day to start becoming the kind of team leader your team deserves? Isn't it time to stop wondering why your last leadership attempt didn't have the desired effect?

Instead, you can be the kind of team leader who others describe as "always focusing on the right problem" and "having the knack of moving her team in the right direction." You can become the team leader that others look up to and hope to emulate.

The leadership concepts presented in this book are proven means that will produce more effective teams and long-lasting results. Organizational psychologists have been taught these concepts since that field began. Dr. Rosner has translated them into a form that current and future leaders can understand and implement immediately.

Each chapter will give you new insights into more effective team leadership. Suggested exercises will solidify your learnings and allow you to practice your new skills while you are leading the team.

Leadership is not solely determined by genes! Leadership is not an inborn set of personality traits! Instead, it is a set of skills to be learned and honed into sharp tools. Get started now in becoming the kind of leader you always wanted to be.

My Personal Preface:

This Book Will Change Your Life:
Its Contents Changed Mine!

When I came to Atlanta to attend Georgia State University in the mid 1960's, I was the stereotypical "wet behind the ears" graduate student, but I thought I was God's gift to the GSU Psychology Department. I came from a Big Ten University (Indiana University) with a well-known and well-lauded psychology department. At the time, the GSU psychology department was small and not very distinguished. They had just been given permission to award a Ph.D. by the school and the American Psychological Association.

It mattered little to me. I wanted to study with a particular professor, who, according to my research, was the best Organizational Psychology Consultant in the world. He had accepted me as one of his students, so off I went to Atlanta.

As a student, I was top-notch – good grades, research skills, dedicated, willing to work hard, and smart. As a person, I was mediocre, at best. Not that I did bad things -- I was brought up with Midwestern values and knowledge of appropriate behavior, so I knew right from wrong and behaved accordingly. But what I eventually realized was that I really didn't know anything about myself.

I had taken philosophy in college and understood Socrates when he opined at his heresy trial that, "The unexamined life is not worth living." I understood it, but I just didn't think it applied to me. There I was, studying to become an organizational psychologist -- an occupation that requires insight into oneself, others, and complex organizations as its starting point -- and yet having pitifully few of these assets at the onset of my career.

I somehow floated along in my student life, taking first year graduate courses and doing well until I encountered my first Group Dynamics course with my major professor. The course was an interacting group rather than a lecture. This was the first course I had taken in which the student didn't passively listen to the professor. The behavior that was studied was also the behavior that was generated in the classroom. In other words, it was not theoretical. It was real. The object of the course was to actually form a team in which everyone participated.

During one session, the "leader," my major professor and the man to whom I had effectively handed responsibility for developing my career, looked at me and said, "Are you angry with me about something?" I truthfully answered, "No," because I felt no anger and was more concerned with why he would say such a thing – especially in front of all my peers.

He insisted that I seemed angry, and after repeated denials, he asked me to "try a little exercise." He placed his back against the concrete block wall of the classroom and extended his arms. He then said, "Grab my hands and try to push me through the wall." My classmates giggled. I put my hands against his and made a feeble attempt to do as he bid. He insisted that I "really try to push him through the wall," and I decided that I would increase my effort a little in an attempt to get this thing over with.

Within a few seconds, I realized two things:
1. *The room had changed from joking and giggles to a tense and absolute silence, and*
2. *I was pushing with every ounce of strength I could muster to actually push him through that wall.*

By the time he called off the exercise, I was perspiring heavily and was exhausted. I sat in my chair heavily and was very confused. It seemed like an eternity before anyone spoke.

The professor, who was also exhausted from "fending me off," looked at me and said, "Perhaps I was right about there being some anger there." Everyone roared with laughter.

A shocking revelation came when I finally asked myself, "How could I be so angry at my major professor and NOT KNOW IT?" It must have been a visible emotion, because he saw it. He understood what would happen when I took part in the "little exercise." Yet I was totally blind to it. In retrospect, I realized that my behavior was a young man's general rebellion against authority. At the time, however, I was blindsided by my own behavior.

This was the most dramatic event up to that point in my life. It brutally forced me to face two truths:

First, I was totally ignorant about my internal self. I had never really asked the question of myself, "Why did I do that?" I didn't know how to look beyond the rationalizations that the first answer typically produces. I had almost no ability to generate self-insight. That was scary!

Second, in order to become a competent psychologist, I knew that I needed to develop that set of skills, both for my personal benefit and also to use in understanding other people and organizations.

When I finally became aware of this tremendous lack of understanding of why I behaved as I did, I also realized the handicapping nature of that missing information. How could I correct problems and improve myself if I didn't recognize the problems in the first place? I recognized a universal truth:

Correct identification of a problem is the first step in resolving it.

You can be aware that things aren't going well for you, but that is not the same as identifying the cause. The signs that things aren't going well are symptoms of the problem. You can correct the symptoms time and again, but until the cause is identified, understood, and corrected, little progress will be made. That single act of opening my eyes to my real problem allowed me to become a better person and a better professional.

That event marked the starting point of a lifelong effort to try to understand myself and the people and groups around me. Fortunately for me, my chosen field of organizational psychology contains many tools designed to help in developing insight into both the self and others.

Over the course of my career, it has been that hard-won insight and the ability to use those tools in the service of the individuals and companies that I have been proud to serve that have led me to write this book.

THIS MATERIAL CAN CHANGE YOUR LIFE TOO.

"Ignorance is bliss." You hear this a lot, but it isn't true. Ignorance is a nightmare. Walking around your world not knowing what is really happening around you is like playing "Pin the Tail on the Donkey" while wearing a blindfold all day long, every day. The idea of walking around in ignorance, not seeing the potential stumbling blocks directly in your path sends chills down my spine. My book will help you blast through such ignorance with newfound knowledge. This book will:

- Help you recognize those things right in front of you and that have always been there – you just never saw them before.
- Teach you how to develop an understanding of what you see.
- Allow you to move your work team in the right direction and increase their effectiveness.
- Most important, it will empower you to become a more effective leader.

Awareness of Your World

Regardless of how much management knowledge you acquire and how many management skills you master -- if you are unaware of what is actually happening in your work team, it is unlikely that your leadership interventions will work well. This awareness is critical to focusing your actions in order to create an effective work team.

It doesn't take a Ph.D. in Psychology to be aware that every day we hear of people who act "crazy." They behave in a way that defies logic or even predictability. Watch a newscast -- almost any newscast. Mothers kill their babies, fathers abuse their children, and students receive a poor grade on their report cards and then attack their teachers.

More than a decade ago, I received a life-extending kidney transplant because in an incident on an interstate highway, a motorist was shot and subsequently died after driving between two cars in which the drivers were shooting at each other. He lived several hours on life-support and his family donated his organs to several people on the organ waiting list. I was one of the donor recipients. Think about how crazy, not to mention how improbable, that situation was. Someone died in a freak accident and he was an organ donor—for me and for others.

Understanding human behavior takes effort, but it is well-worth the time devoted to it. Even when daily situations are more "normal," understanding why people behave as they do can be perplexing. It is not unusual to hear that little voice in your head saying, "I wonder why I just did that." If you often don't understand why you do things, consider how much more difficult it is to understand the behavior of others.

It must be noted that real-world managers rarely receive formal training in how to manage their subordinates. It is also rare that a company has a formal management style that is taught and expected to be used by all of its managers.

In the work situation, people are often interdependent. As a manager, it is difficult to be an effective "coach" of subordinates if you don't understand why:

1) Your subordinate is not performing well
2) Your first corrective suggestion did not work,
3) The second (3rd, etc.) corrective attempt did not work, or
4) The threat of termination was insufficient to bring about behavior change.

To improve performance and move people toward effective behavior, the manager must perform three distinct steps:

1. **"SEE"** what behavior is happening,
2. **"UNDERSTAND"** the rationale for the behavior,
3. **"GUIDE the team"** – Intervene in a way that encourages the person to behave more effectively.

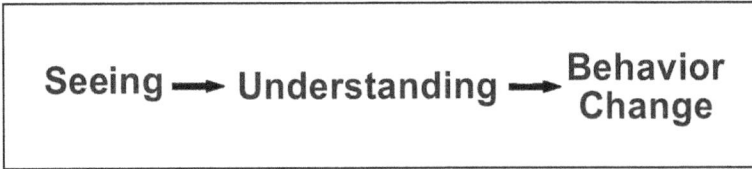

Seeing ➞ Understanding ➞ Behavior Change

Of these, the most important step is the observation of the behavior. When a team is not getting the job done, there is more happening than merely poor performance. The employee is doing something other than performing well. As we will discuss later, it is unlikely that the employee knows why he is not doing what he could do effectively. (If he knew, he would probably self-correct the behavior.) The manager must learn to see what the employee is actually doing and understand his motivation (or lack of it).

In addition, timeliness is critical. Making an observation and commenting on it an hour after it occurs, minimizes the effectiveness. Instead, a much more instantaneous response is needed when the behavior is observed, whether that response is praise or corrective action.

However, if the behavior is unseen, there will be no attempt to understand why it occurred. Similarly, there will be no attempt to conceive of a more productive way to behave. Finally, if the leader does not see the behavior, understand it, and try to picture what the more appropriate behavior would have been, there will be no reason to attempt an intervention to change the behavior.

Leadership INSIGHT is the first step that leads to the initiation of the next two. But you may be asking yourself, "Why would I not see what is happening before my eyes?"

Our World and How We See it

Humans are not normally aware of everything that is going on around them. If you were aware of everything going on in your immediate environment, your brain couldn't handle the ensuing chaos. All of us are constantly bombarded by sights, sounds, smells, etc. In order to deal with our world, we all selectively perceive those signals that seem to be the most relevant.

When watching television, you can become engrossed in a program, but a whiff of smoke or a baby's cry or a telephone ring can instantly break that concentration. Both the ability to focus and the ability to recognize important extraneous signals are primitive defense mechanisms. They have helped humans survive for millennia.

In today's high tech environment, there can be distractions that focus our attention to the point where we can "override" these defense mechanisms. In some cases, people become so engrossed in texting their friends while driving a car that they crash the car. The conversation was more diverting to them than actually paying attention to their immediate environment. Fortunately, in most cases these defense mechanisms remain operational.

Most non-human animals also have similar mechanisms that aid their survival. What separates humans from those other animals is that most of the time we routinely see and understand multiple layers of such signals simultaneously. This is especially true when you are trained and you choose to do so.

One of the most common occurrences when I am introduced as a psychologist to others in informal social situations is the question, "Are you analyzing me right now?" In response, I have learned to smile and reply, "Not unless you are paying me." This usually brings a chuckle to all concerned, not to mention a quiet sigh of relief from the questioner.

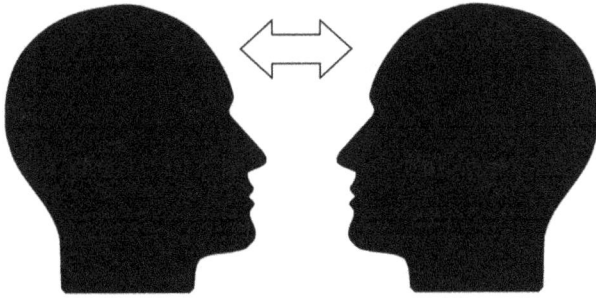

What I am actually saying without words is, "There is a lot of work involved in 'turning on' those tools I use to analyze the behavior of others. Doing analysis is difficult and energy consuming. It is work, not something I do recreationally."

PSYCHOLOGISTS DON'T READ MINDS.

There is a misconception that is widespread in our population that somehow, psychologists can see inside people and read their minds. This myth may be believed because people who have been exposed to applied psychologists (clinical, counselling, industrial, organizational, etc.) often are surprised at the accurate insights these psychologists communicate. It appears that we psychologists are able to draw correct conclusions with little or no data. It may also appear as if we are mind-readers. But I guarantee that there are no academic courses in mind-reading in psychology graduate schools. Instead, we intuit the thoughts of others from their behavior.

Psychologists "Read" Behavior

Graduate training in psychology includes training in the close observation of behavior and learning to interpret that behavior. The latter requires understanding of the breadth and depth of what is considered to be "normal" behavior.

Many people "see" behavior, but in most cases, they "go on to the next thing." In contrast, I was trained to ask questions about the behavior I observed. The leader of a team also should learn to ask relevant questions about what is going on among his team members.

For example:

- What does this behavior mean?
- Why is it present now?
- What caused it?
- How is it connected to what happened before?
- How is it connected to what has been just said?
- Does it "make sense" given the situation?

The answers to these questions will allow the leader to develop a deeper understanding of what the group is doing and to focus on what is happening now and why. When leaders look at the behavior of their group in this way, they can see more clearly what needs to be changed in order to help the group become more effective and successful. The more data that is collected and the more questions answered, the more likely that a good level of understanding will develop. As understanding increases, your interventions to improve the team will become more successful.

Words are Just One Type of Behavior.

I was trained to look "beyond the words" that are spoken and observe other behaviors like body position, tone of voice, facial expression, nervousness, etc. I was also trained to "hear" what was NOT said. For example, I might ask myself, what would this kind of conversation "normally" contain that is now missing? Which topics are being avoided? What sounds "out of place here?"

The answers to these questions are each data points. Each is used to formulate hypotheses about what is causing the behavior and to develop potential ways to correct that behavior. Hypotheses are "stored," awaiting additional evidence that helps to accept or reject each hypothesis. Many are discarded – few get supported.

Data points don't appear as flashing neon signs over someone's head telling us what is wrong and how to correct it. (As helpful as that sounds!) Instead, they are suggestions as to where to look for further answers. They are guides toward a deeper understanding of cause and effect in a particular situation.

Understanding develops much as a photograph develops in the old-fashioned photo lab, getting clearer over time until a clear image appears. As your understanding increases, you become a better guide for the person or group to allow them to "see for themselves" what is going on within themselves or within the group and to allow them to decide whether they want to change that behavior. Awareness enables better choices.

Seeing is Understanding

The psychologist helps the person understand what their words or their behavior means. As a person develops an understanding of why she behaves as she does (self-insight), self-correction is almost automatic.

The primary point is this: When a person "sees" and understands their behavior, the behavior change is already well-started. As British nannies have been intoning for generations, "Well begun is half done." This means that when people try to change their behavior, understanding why they have been behaving as they have been is the more difficult of the two halves of understanding behavior and changing it.

IN THE WORKPLACE

In the workplace, psychological principles are applied to groups as well as to one's self. The hard part is seeing what is happening. If the leader sees what the team is doing, this provides the opportunity to analyze the group behavior and develop the insight necessary for more effective leadership.

You can learn to understand the complexity of the behavioral world in front of your eyes, and understand it better. By understanding it better, you can take action to affect those behaviors and improve the outcomes that you seek.

WHAT IS LEADERSHIP INSIGHT?

Leadership INSIGHT is not one of the five senses, although it can involve using all of them. There are many poor leaders with 20/20 vision. The concept of not being able to "see" what is right before your eyes is not foreign to most people. A person can focus so intently on a task that they fail to notice other factors happening at the same time.

This is a different situation from not seeing the famous "500 pound gorilla" in the room. That particular situation refers to something going on that everyone knows about but refuses to acknowledge. In this case, however, there is a covert agreement to avoid the topic. Everyone "sees" it, but prefers to pretend that it is not there. This is usually caused by the fear of what would happen if such an acknowledgment and a conversation about it actually occurred.

> *In an art class, the professor used the word "chiaroscuro" (the use of strong contrasts between light and dark). From the moment he explained the word and how artists use the effect, I have never been able to see a painting without noticing it.*

The purpose of this book is to "open your eyes" to the complex weave and multiple levels of behavior that are happening, and have always been happening in your work team. As you read through each chapter, you may be surprised by the richness and complexity that becomes apparent.

While the primary purpose of this book is the application of these techniques in the workplace, the same principles apply in all groups. Your Leadership INSIGHT can also be applied in community groups, church groups, family groups and even to groups of two. It is a very powerful tool.

While it can take years of training to become a professional at seeing, understanding, and learning how to change behavior, this is not the goal of this book. Instead, I have selected a number of key factors which, for the most part, are secrets taught in most psychology graduate schools. When understood (and practiced) they yield high levels of rewards for the team leader. These rewards include:

- A leader who is savvier and more powerful,
- A team which is more effective
- A company that is more profitable.

Phillip E. Rosner, Ph.D.

How to Read This Book:

This book is directed at everyone interested in leading groups of people effectively. Since social scientists typically define groups as having two or more members, that definition includes all management situations except the case where you are managing yourself.

The preface includes information important to the total understanding of these new concepts. It is short and should be read.

If you have had little team management training or experience, you should read the rest of the book in order. A total novice at team management, or someone who has read a little but has minimal practical experience, should have no difficulty with the 12 Secrets if they understand the basics of the first two chapters. For those with more experience, these chapters may serve as a refresher course in the basics of team behavior and team leadership. These two chapters provide context for the 12 Secrets.

You can skip Chapter One if you have a basic understanding of leadership as a field of study and some experience applying it as team manager, or have a clear understanding high-performance teams and championship organizations.

Because Chapter Two defines the term "team," and differentiates between teams, groups, committees, and co-acting groups, it can be skipped if you already understand these differences and how they differ in the workplace.

The material covered in the rest of the book represents the unique viewpoint and learning that organizational psychologists are taught which allows them to see "deeper" into people, teams, and organizations. It is presented in a manner and at a level that any student of team behavior can understand and put to practical use. These concepts are tools to increase insight into what is actually happening in the work team and how to lead the team to more effective behavior.

I hope you enjoy your experience in reading this book. It is presented in the hope of opening your eyes to the world of team functioning.

Chapter ONE
Let's Start at the Beginning

ALL leadership behavior must be preceded by a clear and insightful understanding of what is actually happening in the group.

The majority of leadership books start in the wrong place. They emphasize results to be achieved (profit, return on investment, yearly growth, share of market, etc.). But poor results are actually symptoms of an underlying problem. The symptoms are not the problem itself. It is also true that if leaders don't find out what is causing the problems, they are forced to guess what the cause is and make a change. If it works – great! If it doesn't -- they must try something else. It's like a physician prescribing medication for the runny nose and cough rather than finding out what is causing them. It could be a cold—or pneumonia.

If your quarterly profit and loss statement indicates that your profits are too low, it is not enough to direct your executive team to lower costs and increase prices. That's a nice idea, but much harder to achieve than it is to say. Lowering cost may lead to consequential problems: lower quality, reduced productivity, etc. Likewise, increasing prices may have similar problems associated with your competitiveness, market share, and other issues.

Standard leadership models might tell you to assemble your team and pose the problem to them. Task them with figuring out a way to increase profits. Have them come up with solutions that increase profits. Such a strategy might even be successful. However, it ignores what I think is a more important question: "Why did a well experienced and intelligent executive team end up with such poor results?"

As an organizational psychologist, I step back a bit and ask the question: WHY did the company have an UNEXPECTED lowering of profit? WHY did the team not predict and anticipate this outcome? WHY are we where we are now? Asking "why" is the heart of the concept that people call "insight." As the word implies, it refers to looking inside yourself/team/organization. We do so in order to understand why things happen. Preferably, you can use insight into yourself and your organization to anticipate problems that might happen and prevent them.

Most leadership books do not help their readers to achieve deeper insight into their work teams. It is not enough to teach leaders what to do … one must help leaders see more clearly what is happening, so that they can more effectively decide what is needed.

Deciding what needs to be done is CRITICAL!

"If you don't know where you are going, any road will get you there."
−The Cheshire Cat to Alice -
Alice in Wonderland (Lewis Carroll,)

How to get things done is the focus of most leadership books. Of course, leaders must focus upon goals. However, the most clever, ingenious, and original intervention into the life of the team by its leader is worthless unless it is aimed at the right problem. The leader's choice of what to target is the critical decision. If the wrong target is selected, it doesn't matter how well you carry out the attempt at change. You may change the team, but not solve the problem. Conversely, if the right target is selected, the change attempt is much more likely to be effective. It is at that point that application of your preferred leadership philosophy and style comes into the picture. Let's start with a typical example:

Imagine yourself as the newly appointed leader of a new work team in a new (to you) company. This is your first day on the job and you know none of the people in the conference room. No one in their right mind would start the session by issuing order after order to the people, and then asking/stating "Are there any questions?" and leaving the room.

It doesn't take an expert in leadership to know that you need more information about the team, the people in the room, their history with each other, their track record, and a dozen other factors before you know enough to tell them what to do. In actuality, new leaders tend to sit back and collect data before issuing orders. They take time to get to know their team members. They let the team members know how they operate. They tell them their expectations and goals. All of this is good... but it is still not enough!

One reason this book exists is because most new leaders (as well as most seasoned leaders) don't do this well.

Most managers are handicapped because their:

- Data collection tends to be cursory
- Observational skills are limited by their failure to understand the complexity of the team environment and of their team
- Ability to understand what motivates a particular team member is rudimentary
- Knowledge of multiple ways to change the behavior of their employees and teams is severely limited

One should not blame a leader for being unskillful at something of which they are unaware. Neither should they be blamed for areas in which they have never been trained.

The goal of this book is to equip new and experienced leaders with the tools for understanding what is happening in their work teams. These tools work whether applied to the lowest level team in a factory or the senior executive team in a multi-national corporation. Parenthetically, these tools are equally effective in not-for-profit groups and one-on-one interactions.

LEADERSHIP IS TEAM

It makes little sense to talk about leadership without taking into account the people to be led. A leader with no followers is not really a leader. To sit alone in the room, giving orders to nonexistent people is not leadership. All leadership behavior is supposed to be purposeful and directed at people, and it takes place in some context. Let's look at that situation.

LEADERSHIP IS BEHAVIOR

Leadership is the sum of the interventions attempted in the work life of an individual or a group in order to influence them toward a certain direction. (Intervention is defined, for our purposes, as the decision to act or intentionally refrain from acting.) Because leadership is an attempt to influence others, its natural measurement involves whether that influence is successful.

Most books on leadership focus on knowledge and values. They try to tell the reader what good leadership looks like. Some of them seem to say, "Do what I do," and suggest you model your behavior after theirs. Some of them say, "Do the opposite of what I did," and avoid their mistakes.

Conveying knowledge to people in the form of books is relatively safe for authors. If they present something that the reader already knows, no real harm is done. That knowledge is just reinforced. If the underlying values are discussed and the readers do not agree with them, they are not bound to adopt those values.

LEADERSHIP BEHAVIOR IS A SKILL

Advocating certain leadership behavior is a completely different issue – its application has consequences. As a skill, leadership not only has to be learned, it has to be practiced, assessed for effect, modified if necessary, and re-tried until perfected. A set of leadership behaviors that works in one situation might have the opposite effect in another.

Because leadership behaviors are typically not organized into any system, people get confused as to which leadership intervention to use in which situation. Effective intervention is a difficult skill to learn and practice.

When I first started my practice, there were only a few people in the world who knew how to do team-building. Participants would often experience great changes brought about after relatively simple interventions by the group trainer. These were highly skilled professionals who made it look easy.

In fact, it looked so easy that a surprisingly large number of people apparently thought, "I can do that!" They were enthusiastic because they had witnessed the power of a particular intervention. Their enthusiasm was attractive to potential clients and many companies hired these individuals to do team-building. The goals of team-building were desirable; however, these non-trained professionals did not know how to bring about those changes.

Gradually a team-building fad emerged, frequently populated by trainers who were poorly trained (if at all). This plethora of ineffective trainers resulted in team-building efforts that were expensive and unsuccessful --- and eventually caused the fad to die out. It also gave a negative connotation to the term "team-building".

I have come to understand that the most appropriate focus of a leadership book should be on understanding the situation and the people involved before focusing on what to do. In my professional practice, I have consistently discovered that the most effective leaders seem to intervene successfully when they completely understand the people involved and the situation. As the understanding of what is really happening increases, the selection of an intervention becomes easier and has more of a tendency to be effective.

UNDERSTANDING MUST PRECEDE LEADERSHIP BEHAVIOR

In my role as an executive advisor, I frequently hear the words:

> *"Can you help me to solve a problem I am having with my people? My attempts to fix the situation have failed."*

I usually ask a set of questions to clarify my understanding of all of the situation's variables.

One time, a vice president who I was advising asked me, "Why don't you ever answer my question directly? You always ask me a lot of questions. Isn't there a correct answer?"

His statement surprised me, and I hesitated for a moment. I confronted him directly and said, "Of course not! There are dozens, if not hundreds, of answers to your question. It depends on the people, the situation, your subordinate's goals, your corporate goals, the kind of person you are, the kind of person your subordinate is, the kind of culture your company has, your history with that subordinate, and numerous other variables. The more variables you take into account, the more likely it is that your intervention will be successful."

It has always been my secret desire that leading people and groups would be simpler. It would be nice to have a dozen or two standard answers that fit all leadership situations and variables. That, however, is not the way the real world operates. There is a lot that a potential leader needs to know before he or she applies their knowledge of leadership. That conversation, early in my career, started my thought processes about those things that develop leadership knowledge and values. This book is a direct result of that dialogue.

AWARENESS MUST PRECEDE UNDERSTANDING

Becoming aware of yourself and others, of how people and groups interact with each other and of how to intervene to improve the functioning of all relevant parties, is a continuous lifelong goal. It entails developing Leadership INSIGHT – "new eyes" that allow you to see what is really happening in front of you. It involves developing better understandings of how people interact with each other. It involves changing some of the social niceties which dictate "not to see or hear" what you have just seen or heard. More will be said about this later in the book.

I will be presenting and discussing twelve concepts involved in developing Leadership INSIGHT. They have the common purpose of helping you develop new ways of observing what has always been there. As you learn each concept, you will recognize that you could have seen these things working before -- you just didn't.

It is surprisingly easy to add these concepts to your repertoire. Some of them will be added with little more work than describing their existence. Some will take some time for you to fully appreciate. Where appropriate, I have proposed exercises to illustrate the concept and increase your skill in using it. The examples are designed to be used in your work world with your team members. They are practical exercises, rather than theoretical ones.

This Awareness is Permanent

Once you have developed Leadership INSIGHT, it cannot be un-learned. Learning to open your eyes and see what is directly in front of you quickly becomes second nature and cannot be discarded. Whether you are in a group of two people or twenty people, you will never see that group in the same way as you did before. You always retain the choice to not intervene in the life and functioning of that group, but you will no longer have the choice to remain unaware of what is happening.

I believe it is better to see what is really happening in your world than to be oblivious to it. Leadership INSIGHT will open your eyes to the complexities in your world. As I said in the introduction, "Ignorance is not bliss."

Phillip E. Rosner, Ph.D.

Chapter TWO
What is a leader?

It's easy to become a leader! Start your own business, assemble a team, and appoint yourself the leader. Now, wasn't that easy? No experience necessary! No track record necessary! No skills necessary! Tell your team what to do, and then fire them if they don't do it. If your team obeys your orders but doesn't perform -- get rid of them and hire new people. You're still the leader. Easy – but neither realistic nor effective.

BECOMING AN *EFFECTIVE* LEADER IS NOT SO EASY.

Effectiveness means that your team gets the job done – and done well. Only two things are necessary to achieve the title "Effective Leader": The team must be successful and they must follow you. That's not the same as obeying orders. Some people refer to this as leading from "in front." You show them the way to go, and they follow. Some skills are required, but being the Boss helps a lot. Sometimes things just happen.

A friend of mine played high school football in a "big school" league (4,000 to 5,000 students each). They managed to become the league champions, and the coach won "Coach of the Year." Two things occurred which made this situation quite unusual.

First, none of the seniors who played on the team received football scholarships to any college. Next autumn, a local newspaper even wrote a small article about how unusual that was. The members of the team knew that there were no stars on the team -- just guys who played very well together as a team. When one guy on the team was over-matched by an opponent, they would help each other. Their motivation was simple: "Today, YOU need help – perhaps, next game, I will need the help."

The second unusual situation wasn't known until years later, after the coach retired. He never won another championship. Though he coached for another twenty years, the best any of his teams ever did was third place.

How does one explain this set of occurrences? The old saying is: Even a blind squirrel finds an occasional acorn. That seems to be what happened in this case. As mentioned above, the group played as a real team -- they continuously looked at the immediate situation, assessed it, and adjusted to correct any weaknesses. They found temporary fixes that overcame those weaknesses.

The coach didn't play much of a role in this team development, beyond teaching the team members the basics of playing their positions and calling the plays. His emphasis was always on each player developing himself to his maximum capability. "If you each become as good as you can be -- we will win." His clear emphasis was on team members each playing as high-performing individuals. But the coach didn't have a systematic method of preparing his teams to play as a single unit, or any method that could be repeated every new season. Perhaps that is why he never repeated with another championship team.

I have asked hundreds of people about this phenomenon and discovered that it is not all that rare. A significant number of people have reported being on a sports team or a work team that just clicked. Most report it as a kind of magical experience, and could speak about it, quite extensively and in detail. Of course, it is not magic, it just feels that way.

BECOMING AN EFFECTIVE LEADER WHO BUILDS A CHAMPIONSHIP ORGANIZATION IS EVEN MORE DIFFICULT!

The question that really matters is: *Can a group of people form a working team that repeats its successes year after year?* The answer, of course, is already known – sure they can. We see it in sports with teams winning year after year (e.g. – the New York Yankees and the Atlanta Braves' 15 year winning streak). Their dynasties don't last forever, but they continue for a significant period of time. We also see continued success in the business world in corporations that seem to stay Number One in their respective industries, year after year.

Building a championship team, one that remains at the top of their field, requires a leader who understands what it takes to build a continuously winning team and who insists on nothing less. It also requires some knowledge of how teams operate and some understanding of how to make those conditions happen. In addition, building a championship team that stays on the top requires that the leader develops methods to guide the team and motivate them toward improvement.

This kind of success also requires a set of skills that are rarely taught in business schools and rarely are learned in the real world. I call this Leadership INSIGHT. In the same sense that insight is the process of seeing, recognizing, and understanding *why you behave as you do* -- Leadership INSIGHT is the process of seeing, recognizing, and understanding *why your work group behaves as it does*. These are potentially the most powerful set of skills in the manager's arsenal.

Leadership INSIGHT is the ability to:

SEE: The ability to be aware of what is happening in your workgroup,

UNDERSTAND: The knowledge to understand the significance of that behavior, and

GUIDE the team: The skills to intervene in a way that corrects and redirects the team toward its goals and the confidence to model leadership behavior that encourages the team members to become self-correcting.

Every manager wants to redirect their team when they think it is going off course. Unfortunately, training in this area is minimal. So most team leaders rely on their personal style of management to dictate what they do about it. They most frequently use meeting facilitation skills to get the team back on course.

Such action is often guided by simple ideas like:

- Stay focused
- Avoid going off on tangents
- Keep ideas flowing
- Don't let one person dominate the conversation
- Don't get side-tracked
- Keep to the agenda
- Look for the compromise position
- Discourage conflict
- Address personality issues outside the group.

However, the obvious fallacy in these ideas is that *each idea tries to change the symptom of poor group interaction, rather than attempting to find out why the problem interaction occurred and then correcting the underlying problem.* It avoids that problem rather than fixes it -- in the hope that avoidance will allow the team to maneuver around the problem.

For example, even the best team will occasionally go off on a tangent. But when it happens frequently, something is wrong. There is typically a reason for the tangential behavior. If the team leader (or one of its members) does not find out what is causing the tangential behavior, then the problem will continue. It may even escalate.

My favorite example of intentional tangential behavior occurred in graduate school. Everyone in the class thought the material was boring. The professor hated teaching the subject. Each class session started the same way:

The professor would start his lecture and would continue for a minute or two until one of the students would sense an opening for a tangential question and raise his hand.

The question would typically start with something like, "How does this relate to XYZ"? (XYZ would be one of several fields of psychological research that were hot buttons for this professor. Alternatively, it could be a question about something he was personally involved with at the time (giving blood for pay, or building his new house).

The professor would spend the next 20 to 40 minutes off on a tangent, speaking about something about which he really cared. The professor was enjoying himself and the class was hearing an enthusiastic monolog rather than a boring one.

The class and the professor had entered into a tacit collusion to not cover the lecture material. As I look back on this rather foolish endeavor, I am certain that the class was aware of what was happening, but I am not so certain that the professor was.

For a work team, tangential behavior can be a form of the avoidance of discussing issues that are sensitive or in some way perceived as too difficult to discuss. As mentioned earlier, all work teams go off on a tangent occasionally. It is when that behavior repeats itself sufficiently to harm the overall effort that it becomes problematic. If the leader sees the behavior and understands it, change can be brought about in a rather simple and direct manner.

This book teaches leaders at all levels and in all kinds of organizations to develop Leadership INSIGHT. These concepts will allow them to see and understand what is happening in the group, and enable them to diagnose and improve team behavior, in order to improve team performance.

DEVELOPING A WORKING DEFINITION OF TEAM

A number of years ago, a large aerospace engineering firm was forming a team of senior engineers to look at what future trends they foresaw that might change the strategy of their company. Every engineer in the room had different specialties and all had 10+ years with the firm. They also all had some level of experience working with the other members occasionally over those years. My task was to help them become a team faster than normal. I asked, "You are the Future Trends Team, -- are you a team?"

Thus, they started the initial process of self-analysis on a group level. There is minimal difficulty in understanding that a group is an identifiable assemblage of people.

Five thousand people sitting in a stadium to watch a football game are a group.

Ten people in an elevator are a group. A million people in Times Square in New York City on New Year's Eve are a group.

All three examples are groups, but none of them are teams. They are identifiable, because they have assembled for a reason (to see a game, to move to higher floors in a building, to celebrate New Year's Eve). But it takes more than getting together for a common purpose to make them a team.

Is a Committee a Team?

Committees meet the definition of a group, and they also have a purpose. They are usually formed to produce a product of some kind (a report, a plan of action, a list of candidates, a piece of legislation, and so on). To accomplish that purpose, they will have to work in concert with one another. At first glance, a committee appears to be more than just a group – but it is not.

Committees are frequently composed of members who are representatives of other groups with different agendas. *As a result, for committee members, their goals tend to be external to the committee.* ("I want to make sure that *our* group gets its share of what is being distributed.")

A committee doesn't fit the definition of a team, because its members co-act, but any co-operation that occurs is always colored by each member's desire to represent their external constituency and the best possible outcome for those individuals. It is more competitive than cooperative.

In Washington, D.C., when the House of Representatives and the Senate pass different versions of the same bill, it is sent to a Reconciliation Committee. Only the politically naive believe that this committee is working to produce the most effective bill possible. Instead, it is understood that the resultant law will be a series of compromises in which each side gets the most it can obtain out of the effort. It is the product of a system in which every member of the committee is elected by constituents who expect their representative to maximize their interests.

In contrast, a team's members co-operate to help each other and the group to achieve the overall goal in a non-competitive manner. With teams, each individual member may have their own personal agendas, but they subordinate them to achieve the team's goals.

Is a Group of Insurance Agents a Team?

The general agent of our city's largest insurance agency called and told me that, "Tom X (a client of mine) recommended you, and I need you to work your magic on my team of agents. Cost is no object." These are words that a consultant loves to hear.

But after a few questions I politely turned down his request. I explained to my caller that, while I would be more than happy to have his agency as a client, team building in this case was unlikely to have a significant effect.

I explained that his group was not a team. They were a collection of independent individuals who independently try to maximize their own performances. If one of the agents failed to perform during a given fiscal quarter, it had no effect on the other agents' performances. (This is true, even if that lack of performance might affect a collective bonus.)

There are some groups that are identifiable as a unit (like his group of insurance agents), have a common goal (to have a profitable insurance agency) and are minimally competitive with one another. They are still not a team. They are a co-acting group. They do their jobs independently from each other.

The ultimate test of this situation is to ask each person, "If the person sitting next to you stops doing her job for the next month, how will that affect your monthly performance?" If the answer is that it will have a minimal effect, then you are not truly interdependent in your group. You do not need your colleague to be successful in order for you to be successful. You are not a team.

HOW A TEAM DIFFERS FROM OTHER GROUPS

The key elements that make a team more than a group are collaboration, synergy, a team philosophy, interdependence, shared responsibility and rewards, and the building of a work environment.

Collaboration

A team assembles people with different knowledge, skills, values and approaches, and blends them into a new combination that maximizes the use of those attributes. They are there to work together (co-labor) to achieve the team's goals.

Synergy

The output that a team generates is greater than the sum of the inputs (commonly represented as $1 + 1 = 3$). The team's effort is coordinated and cooperative. It tries to build on whatever has come before and improve the team's output. Everyone works toward that goal.

A Team Philosophy

With a team, the members believe in the superiority of their interaction together. Each member of the team comes to understand and appreciate that the decisions of the team, when arrived at through an appropriate, non-competitive process, are more effective than any decision that one of them could make. It is this knowledge that provides the motivation to continue teaming.

Interdependence

An effective performance from your fellow team members is not merely a nice thing; it is a critical condition in order for you to achieve your goals. If they don't get their job on the team done, or are late in doing so, it makes it more difficult or impossible for you to get your job done or done on time. An attitude of indifference to their plight results in your own failure.

Shared Responsibility and Rewards

In a world where individual reward for individual achievement is the norm, a team is distinguished by the sharing of both. If the team fails, its members fail. In business, being the best member of a team that fails is no honor. Team incentives and rewards provide the impetus to work toward effective teaming.

The Building of a Work Environment

The essence of the goals of team building is developing an environment in which each member's diversity is prized and appreciated, different opinions are seen as valuable, and each member does what he or she can to help every member to maximize their potential.

The senior engineers alluded to at the beginning of this chapter finally decided to use the following definition of team:

A team:

- *Always has a common goal or mission,*
- *Generates synergy through a coordinated, cooperative effort,*
- *Has members who help one another in a non-competitive manner*
- *Has members who are interdependent with regard to accomplishing that goal,*
- *Shares responsibility for the achievement of that goal or for its failure, and*
- *Creates an environment in which all members can maximize their potential.*

We will use their definition for our purposes.

WHAT IS A CHAMPIONSHIP TEAM?

A championship team is a high-performance team that maintains its performance level year after year. They understand what teamwork looks like and realize the value of managing teamwork correctly. They are proud of being such a team year after year. They enjoy setting the standards of performance in their industry. Members of a championship team know that they are at the top of their game and they revel in that knowledge.

WHY ARE HIGH-PERFORMANCE TEAMS BETTER?

High performance teams are better. Why? Because a high-performance team is more than the sum of its parts. Its limits are as high as the team chooses to reach.

On the other hand, a poorly functioning team is limited in what it can accomplish, especially in areas that require cooperation, coordination, intricate strategy, and collaboration.

Here are some of the other reasons why you want to strive to create and maintain a high-performance team:

1. High-performance teams report less stress and more enjoyment when solving complex problems together as compared with when individuals try to solve these problems by themselves.

2. When things must be coordinated, especially among multiple departments, high-performance teams manage this coordination better.

3. As decisions become more complex and long-range, difficult issues are easier to deal with and solutions are better monitored for effectiveness by a high-performance team.

4. Interpersonal issues, difficulties, and interdepartmental conflicts can typically be better resolved (especially in the long-term) by a high-performance team.

5. More ideas are generated by high-performance teams. New and innovative solutions are explored more freely and rejected out-of-hand less frequently.

6. Team functioning becomes a lifestyle not just a current fad. It is an approach to problem-solving and a management technique which, when mastered, makes your corporate life much easier.

The Leader is the Key to Developing a Championship Team

During the process of an executive team-building program at a telecommunications client, the group confronted the Vice President, their boss, about her insistence on superior performance. "We have 32 objective measures of our unit's performance compared to others in our company and we are consistently ranked at the top," noted one of her subordinate directors, "Isn't that good enough?".

The VP looked stunned as she replied, "No! Of course not. We are the best today. If we rest on our laurels, we will not be the best tomorrow. I look at it this way -- every time we set a new standard for excellence, we need to do two things:

First, we need to celebrate. We accomplished what no unit has done before and we deserve to be rewarded.

Second, we set a new and higher goal for tomorrow. There is no set-in-concrete achievement level at which we can say, 'OK, now we can ease off.'

We are the best! We are the stars of the company! The only way to stay there is to continually set new and higher objectives for ourselves. If you don't feel this way -- If you feel like your past performance is the best you can ever do -- then you are on the wrong team."

The VP did not sound like a cheerleader. Instead, she sounded like a committed professional who thought of herself and her team as the New York Yankees of her company. She saw her goal of being a championship team year after year as the only appropriate objective. She wasn't there to play the game; she was there to win it.

If you are ready to develop into the kind of leader that strives for and produces high-performance teams year-after-year, then it is time to:

- Move to the next level
- See what is happening in your team as they function
- Understand what makes your team successful
- Use that understanding to lead your team more effectively
- Learn how to guide and motivate your team
- Develop Leadership INSIGHT

Phillip E. Rosner, Ph.D.

Chapter THREE
SEE What is happening

The secrets you will learn about in this book are rarely taught to the general public. You will learn these secrets here so you will open your eyes to what is and always has been there. The idea of seeing what is happening right in front of you may seem simple, but it is not! There is a general tendency in people to mind their own business – even when it IS their own business.

In fact, often people teach themselves NOT to see what is happening.

If you are in a public place and overhear a couple arguing about something, you probably act like most people do -- as if you really don't hear what they were saying. Privacy is a highly valued commodity.

Another example: Your wife asks you, "Does this dress make me look fat?" Only the dumbest of the dumb husbands believe that she wants an honest critical fashion opinion. The right answer is, "Of course not, honey! You look great!"

Because people often feel like what's going on in front of them is not their business, they don't practice evaluating things at a deeper level. It is socially more appropriate to focus on the surface issues, so you don't train yourself to look beneath the surface. You don't want to intrude. You intentionally do not see.

For the effective leader, this behavior pattern needs to be reversed, and the goal of this chapter is to help you start the reversal process. This chapter covers three secrets designed to open your eyes to how people operate and what makes them do what they do. In order to observe what people do alone and in groups, you need to understand a little about:

- The psychology of how people interact with each other
- What is happening in addition to what is seen, and
- The complexity of behavior and the need to look at several things happening at once.

As a team leader (or potential team leader), nothing is more important than being aware of what is happening in your team.

This section will illustrate that a great deal happens in team meetings that either no one sees or that no one sees at a level that allows them to do something about it.

The first secret is THE law of Psychology (generally known as the Law of Reinforcement). I capitalize THE because there are numerous theories, beliefs, axioms, and ideas in the field of psychology, but the word "law" implies that it happens all of the time. The law of reinforcement is the only one I know of that even approaches this level of consistency.

When explained, this law is generally understood by most people. I can't remember ever having a group hear about it and find it difficult to understand or accept as truth. The really effective part of this concept is in its use as a tool to allow the leader (as well as the team members) to have a basis to search for the underlying meaning of the behavior that is displayed by the team or some of its members. Knowledge of this concept will provide a concrete test that can be used to make sense of what has or is happening in the team. Awareness of its existence forces the leader to search for causes until reasonable explanations are discovered.

The second secret, Content vs. Process, may be a revelation to the uninitiated. While both content and process happen simultaneously, most members of the team are unaware of the latter. Sometimes a member or two will get the feeling that something is not quite right about what is happening. However, since they are rarely trained to see and understand these things, they often avoid dealing with them by switching thoughts to something else that they *can* deal with. There is a sort of group awareness of some of these things. We know this because sometimes a group will react to a really bad process. This sometimes looks like a group gasp, or an awkward silence that lasts a second or less before it is skipped over. The group has obviously reacted to something and has a sense that something bad has occurred, but it is not prepared to deal with it.

The third secret, Simultaneous Multiple Levels of Behavior, is an acknowledgement that team behavior, like most interactive behavior, is complex. When you are a participant in a group, there is a tendency to simplify what you see in order to make it easier to understand and to deal with. That is the exact opposite of what you should be doing. The more that you understand that things are happening simultaneously and at different levels, the easier it will be to develop an understanding of what is happening. You can then decide which of the several things are more important than others and decide in what order to deal with them most effectively.

As you read the next three sections, become aware of what has always been there, but has gone unrecognized and therefore, not understood.

Phillip E. Rosner, Ph.D.

Secret 1. THE Law of Psychology (The Law of Reinforcement)

By definition, a law is something that is unvarying and universal in nature and, therefore, allows for prediction. Laws are not common when considering the field of human behavior. Only one law has stood out for decades as a reliable indicator of behavior, namely, the Law of Reinforcement.

The Law of Reinforcement, most often credited to psychologist B.F. Skinner (and his work with Operant Conditioning), is quite simple:

> *Behavior that is reinforced (rewarded) will tend to increase in frequency, while behavior that is punished (with a lack of reward or a punishment) will decrease in frequency.*

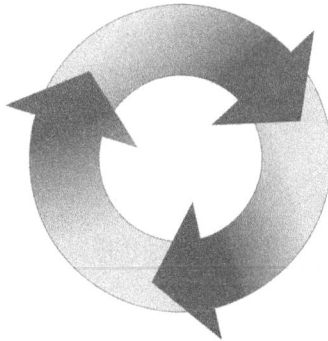

When stated like this, the Law of Reinforcement sounds obvious. Everyone knows that if you rebuke or punish a child (or adult or animal) for a specific behavior, they will tend to do that behavior less frequently. The universality of the law is where its strength lies. It does not require language to work.

Think about "the look" you got from your mother when you did something wrong. No words were needed to know that you were in trouble. Such a signal is universal. It works regardless of your cultural upbringing. It does not have to be taught to work.

The Psychologist's Secret

One of the most valuable tools psychologists have developed is based on this law. It requires that you look at the law somewhat in reverse.

If a behavior is increasing in frequency, it is being rewarded -- and if it is decreasing in frequency, it is being punished.

This restatement of the Law of Reinforcement tells the observer that there is a reinforcement (or a punishment) that is causing the behavior change that will make sense when you discover what it is. The observer (psychologist, team leader, team member, etc.) knows that it is there, so can confidently look for it. When it is found, the behavior will make more sense.

When a person (or a group) does something habitually, it is being rewarded. Your job, as team leader, is to identify and understand that reward. When a person (or a group) fails to learn to do something habitually (or does it less and less frequently) it is being punished. Again, your job is to find and understand that punishment. When that is accomplished, you can look for an appropriate action that will move the person or the group in a more effective direction.

Some will say, what about the child who is constantly acting up? My answer is that the child is likely misbehaving frequently because she is receiving reinforcement for her actions. She may have learned that she usually gets what she wants when she acts up. Also, her goal may be to obtain attention, even if it's negative attention—and throwing a hissy fit in the toy store about a toy she wants Dad to buy is likely to get her plenty of attention. (And may also get her the toy.) Even if it only worked once, the child will remember.)

Let's move on to an example of problematic adult behavior.

> *In a ready-mix concrete operation, the general manager wanted to increase the productivity of the truck drivers. The manager's biggest problem was lateness and absenteeism. A driver who didn't come to work on time or didn't come to work at all reduced the number of concrete deliveries. Fewer deliveries resulted in lower profits.*

> *The manager, Mr. Y., instituted a program of monetary rewards for those drivers who got to work on time each day and had zero absences during the week. Mr. Y also had a series of punishments, the main one being lack of eligibility for overtime pay for any week in which there were absences or tardiness. The lack of over-time eligibility was considered especially strong because it represented a decrease in extra take-home pay of 35% to 75%.*

> *The program failed completely. The drivers who typically had one or more incidents of tardiness and one or more days absent did not improve at all in either category. Because neither reward nor punishment had the desired effect, we decided to interview the errant drivers.*

> *The interviews discovered that both the rewards and the punishments were insufficient to change the drivers' behaviors. While the number of dollars lost was considerable with lateness or absenteeism, the value of a day off from tough physical labor was seen by them as a much stronger reward.*

The lesson learned from this failed attempt to change behavior is that the rewards and punishments must be viewed from the perspective of the person whose behavior you are trying to change. A reward must be more valuable or desirable to the person than *the reward he obtains from exhibiting the habitual behavior.* So you need to look at the problem from his perspective in order to change his behavior. How do you do that? Often by simply asking the person or by having another individual in the company ask him.

During my first job at a mental hospital, a patient asked me to change his work assignment from the cafeteria (typically seen as the best job in the hospital) to the laundry (typically seen as the worst job). Because it seemed so illogical, I asked him to tell me why. He responded that, THEY were putting SOMETHING in the food that caused it to be absorbed THROUGH HIS SKIN and, because of this, he was gaining unwanted weight. I recognized this as a "textbook" set of paranoia symptoms. The patient was behaving based on his (albeit irrational) beliefs.

The mechanism the patient proposed for his weight gain (absorption of the food while carrying the tray to the cafeteria line) was irrational, but given that he believed it, he was asking for a solution of working in the laundry that he believed would ultimately reward him (weight stabilization).

In a group setting, frequently repeated behavior is a sign that the group's behavior is being rewarded. If the person who is trying to figure out what is happening in the group starts from a position that says repeated behavior is being rewarded, changing the reward will typically change that behavior.

In the same way that a detective searches for multiple clues in multiple ways, the team leader must also search in multiple ways. The detective looks at a crime scene and asks, "What is out of place or missing here?" The team leader asks, "What is happening in this group that seems out of place?" or "What seems to be strange or unexpected behavior?" She may also ask, "When I tried to influence the group, why didn't it work?"

Frequently the team leader will see that the group moved in a direction that would not have been predicted. One of the most common results after watching a team interact is the question "Why did that happen?"

When a work team seems to operate in a manner that appears to be less than optimal, it may not even be noticed, at first. In fact, the occurrence of a single incident of such a behavior may not be significant at all. If it is not repeated, it may be one of those random acts that a group (or an individual) may occasionally make. However, if it happens repeatedly, it is being reinforced, and the leader should make an effort to understand what is being reinforced and if it is non-productive behavior, the leader needs to try to redirect the team.

Leadership INSIGHT is greatly increased by the simple step of knowing that all repetitive group behavior either rewards the group or avoids punishment. Confident in that knowledge, the team leader can begin searching for the reward.

Sometimes people's behavior seems – and is – irrational. While working for the Board of Elders in a large church, I witnessed an important discussion about one of two possible actions they could take. The decision would have a significant impact on their parishioners.

When the vote was taken, I saw one board member cast the deciding vote FOR the decision even though I knew he did not actually support that position. We had discussed his position at length and I knew he was against the decision based upon strongly held moral grounds. I could not imagine why he had changed his position so drastically.

After the meeting, I pulled him aside and asked if he had had a change of heart. "No" he said. I asked why he voted opposite of his beliefs. His reply was quite logical to him and yet shocking to me. He said, "John K. was speaking against the change and I'll be G... D...ed if I will let him win a vote on this board!"

Developmental Exercise: The Law of Reinforcement

This exercise will talk about what to do with an individual who is not responding well to an effort to change behavior. Please note that is applies equally well with group behavior.

The example is quite simple. An employee is not doing well at his job. As his manager, you meet with him and explain what he is doing wrong and how to correct the behavior. You check to make sure that he has understood what the problem is, and what the new behavior looks like that you expect to see from him.

In the belief that this should be sufficient, you tell the employee that you expect that he will now correct his behavior. He leaves and you think to yourself, problem solved. But a few days later, you observe that the behavior has not improved. What do you do now?

In my experience, it is quite common for the manager to:

1) Ask why the behavior did not change
2) Get a plausible reason for the lack of change, and
3) Repeat the above scenario, once again telling the employee the problem, and how to correct it. It rarely works any better the second time. In my experience, it is not unusual to see several iterations of this sequence, all with minimal results.

Why the manager repeats behavior that already hasn't worked at all has always concerned me. The communication has already been checked – the desired new behavior has been understood by the employee –why repeat it? I have been able to come up with only two reasons:

1) The manager is being persistent. If at first you don't succeed, try, try again. While I believe in "try, try again", I question the wisdom of re-trying what has already failed.

2) The manager has been unable to think of an alternative method to correct the behavior. My personal belief is that this is the more believable reason.

The following exercise is designed to both look for possible solutions to the current example, and to develop, in the manager, the discipline of applying the Law of Reinforcement. It is based on the most simple of scientific principles, recording observations and using them to know more about the subject. The strength of this exercise is in the fact that you are writing down what you are doing. Over time, you will compile a folder of this material which you can look at to see what works well and what does not. REMEMBER, this exercise is done for the development of your employee and for your development too.

DO NOT do this exercise "in your head". Each step is important and should be written down and done in sequence.

1. Prepare for the Meeting

Think about what you have done in relation to trying to change the employee's behavior:

Record the first attempt to change the employee's behavior. What did you assume was the reason for the poor behavior, what did you do and what was the result? Think about what is being reinforced or punished.

 In writing down this experience, prepare for the second change attempt by asking yourself, "Why didn't this intervention change the employee's behavior?" Then speculate about what you think the actual reason was that the change attempt did not work, and what you will do the next time. Write this down as #1, draw a line under this speculation and think about a conversation in which you try to solve it.

Then say to yourself, "That speculation about the actual reason is incorrect. That's not the reason the intervention didn't change the behavior." Now, think about another possible reason that the change attempt didn't work and what you will do the next time. Write it down as #2, and draw a line under this and think about the conversation in which you try to solve it. Repeat this procedure one more time.

You now have a list of three new possible conversations you can have with the employee. That list is in the order of what you believe to be the most likely reason the employee did not succeed. Consider all three, and make a guess as to which one is most likely to be correct and use it to actually have the next meeting with the employee.

2. Meet with the employee:

Start the discussion by asking the employee why the behavior did not change. Record the answer. Use the conversation you previously decided was most likely to succeed and tell the employee that you will speak again about this. Record the results and wait to see if change occurs.

If the behavior changes, go back to the written record and indicate that your selected choice seems to have worked. Have a conversation with the employee and congratulate them on the successful improvement.

If the behavior change does not occur, ask the employee why there was no change and repeat the process (knowing that none of your reasons were correct). Most important is that you have an internal conversation with yourself as to why you did not understand the motivation of the employee.

3. Repeat until behavior changes or employee is removed

The objective of the exercise is to use the knowledge that all behavior gets changed in accordance with the Law of Reinforcement to help you to increase your ability to predict which management acts will result in behavior change.

The ultimate goal is to increase your skill in discovering what motivates your employee or your team. As this exercise is regularly applied, most managers find that they get better at predicting the causes of behavior, and they see that their correct guess as to why the behavior is happening moves closer and closer to the top of their list.

Use of the Law of Reinforcement by the Team Leader

Leading a team toward high performance involves a complex set of considerations and behaviors. The above exercise is intended to be a simple starting point for the team leader to use when contemplating how to move the team in a desired direction.

In my practice advising leaders of senior executive teams, one of the most common questions they ask me is, "Why did the team do something that made no sense to me? It's absolutely irrational."

The Law of Reinforcement tells the leader that what at first glance may seem irrational must, in reality, be rational to the person exhibiting the behavior. Now you must dig deeper because you don't yet see how this behavior is rewarding the team. *That* is the starting point for developing understanding. The leader knows that there is a *rational* motivation underlying the team's behavior -- the challenge is to find it.

Sometimes all you have to do is ask.

Earlier I described a case in which a long-standing personal grudge against a fellow board member had a greater effect on this person's vote than his own personal beliefs about the direction he felt his church should take. On some internal set of scales, it was more rewarding to keep his fellow board member from being on the winning side of a vote than it would have been to vote his own beliefs.

In the above case, I had the opportunity to ask the person why he did what he did. In many cases, it isn't convenient to do so. When it is convenient --always ask. When it is not, try to postulate a reason that makes some sense to you. Remember, it makes sense to the people involved --- even if it doesn't make any sense to you. Keep trying to find that reason. It is there!

Allow the group to achieve better performance by studying their behavior

As your understanding of how to apply the Law of Reinforcement improves, you will find better and newer ways of interpreting what you see the group doing. One of the basic principles of team leadership is to help *them* understand why *they* behave as they do. Another basic principle to establish is that it is acceptable and appropriate to examine how the group functions and not just to analyze its results. Serendipitously achieved outcomes may pay off in the short run, but solid, well-thought-through effective procedures will pay off consistently in the future.

Secret 2. Content versus Process (Who is doing what, to whom?")

Content

Content, in a group setting, is simply what is being said, stripped of all social cues and all emotionality. Imagine that a group meeting is being recorded. Someone listens to the tape and transcribes that recording to construct a type-script of the proceedings. Those words are the content. The transcript contains no sounds to be interpreted, no facial expressions or body movement to use to understand the words -- just the words.

Of course it does not include the words that were unspoken. To focus on just the words is the equivalent of taking the words at face value and ignoring all other information. It may sound somewhat odd, but choosing to respond to content and ignoring all other data is a common choice for individuals and teams.

For example:

You arrive at your office two hours late and as you are taking off your coat, your boss comments, "Are you just now getting to the office?"

The content is very clear -- a request for information or clarification. If you only respond to the content, you might say, "Correct! You are an accurate observer."

Knowing nothing more than the content of the above scenario, imagine that you are this boss, and (before you read the next few paragraphs) think about how you would respond. As the boss, would you say "Thank you for the compliment. I like to think that I am a proficient observer." Or would you be much more likely to say something else? *Most people would say something else.*

Process

Process is the *subtext* of the words. It happens during the expression of the content and underlies it. It is the answer to the question: "Who is doing what to whom?"

It includes the emotional impact that the words have on the receiver or on the group or the task at hand. Process *always* has an effect on the individual and the group. It also includes the underlying function of the words.

In the above example about the boss questioning you for being two hours late, you had better not miss the subtext. Whether that subtext comes from your boss' tone of voice or the expression on her face, or from the fact that silence enveloped the room instantly as soon as the words were spoken -- it is not merely a request for information. The aforementioned silence in the room (often accompanied by a rapid intake of breath) affirms that everybody knows that more has happened than a mere request for information.

In this case, the underlying message (the process) is more potent than the words actually spoken. The meaning of those words could actually be, "Why are you two hours late for work?" or "This is your third time being late this week!" Your answer should address the underlying process, not the content. *Respond to the content only at your own peril.*

Why didn't my boss just say what she meant?

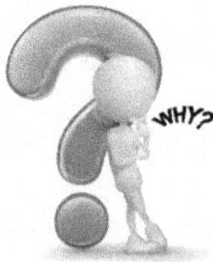

In general, most leaders are sensitive to their relative superiority in rank to their subordinates. If possible, they would prefer to avoid using their power to change a subordinate's less desirable behavior.   In the lateness example, pointing out your repeated tardiness in front of your peers might be seen as an aggressive confrontation in a situation that didn't seem to require such a strong move. Her words told you that your lateness was noted, and the "don't do that again" message was implied, not stated.

Tacit Collusion – another process condition.

Society allows us to make contracts with each other without saying a word.   This is called a tacit collusion -- an unspoken agreement. At times, this is convenient for us and allows us to "play the game." Groups do this quite frequently. We know that the words have different underlying meanings, but it is easy to pretend that they don't -- and respond only to the words. An old-fashioned example:

> *Near the end of a date, the fellow says (with a wink), "How would you like to come up to my apartment and see my collection of etchings?" She responds (with an answering wink), "I love etchings -- Let's go!"*

The content is clear -- It's a conversation about Art. But the process looks more like a dating ritual. It's a tacit collusion to keep the conversation light. No harm done. Both individuals know what each other really mean.

How about this actual example?

> *One of the most frequent events in a groups discussion is the situation where a lively discussion is happening on a problem and one member calls out, "I know what to do ... we should "blah, blah, blah..."*

> *The room goes silent for a few seconds -- followed by an immediate return to the previous discussion--as if the suggestion was never made.*

> *The silence (absence of communication) sends a clear message to the solution proposer: "We reject your idea without even acknowledging it." Of course, the communication by the group has been accomplished without having the awkwardness of actually saying the words, but the message is received and felt. Being ignored altogether is a powerful message.*

What the group does and doesn't do, what is said and what isn't said, tells a lot about what is happening in the group. The solution provider in the above example is less likely to propose another solution than if the silence never occurred.

The group has said nothing. The effort of the proposer was not acknowledged. The suggested solution was not rejected by any member of the group. It would not be unusual for the proposer to feel invisible to the group. In essence, the proposer was punished for making the comment by being ignored. He feels like an outcast, even though nothing was said. That behavior is now less likely to occur again.

The Law of Reinforcement is clearly operative. If the team fails to acknowledge contributions often enough, team members may start to believe that not every contribution is valued. They will start evaluating what they are about to say in their minds ahead of time in order to judge whether the team will value it enough to acknowledge that a contribution has been made. This self-censorship tends to stifle the free flow of ideas and makes participation in such discussions laborious.

Process MUST be discussed.

Most groups do not spend much time discussing the group process. Part of the reason is that many group members are only marginally aware of the process, if they are aware at all. Another part of the reason is that there has been no previously agreed-upon contract to discuss group process. But work groups always develop contracts with one another. They rarely do it consciously and openly, but those contracts exist.

When you enter a group, there is a general (although usually unspoken) set of common sense rules that are followed. Many people think of it as being civilized. You are not allowed to punch or kick people with whom you disagree. People don't reveal their "deepest darkest secrets" to people they have just met or, for that matter, to most "work friends." (Such deep dark secrets are revealed in groups like Alcoholics Anonymous, where there is a "contract" to do exactly that and is an acceptable place to reveal oneself.)

You don't give your full trust to people at work until it has somehow been earned. (It should be noted that distrust is also earned over time.) There is some relatively shallow level of trust that you automatically give to a work colleague, but it is far short of full trust. Since most people are aware that trusting relationships are better and more comfortable than those characterized by distrust, why not give more trust at the beginning of the relationship?

There is an expression in the southern US that goes, "It takes a lot of 'atta boys' to overcome one 'That was stupid.'" It is common, although mostly unintentional, that things are said in a group that hurt peoples' feelings. If it happens and is not acknowledged, those hurt feelings will fester. It is not unusual to see them show up later in the group's life in a much more virulent form. If they are discussed when they occur, dealt with and resolved, they tend to disappear.

Unfortunately, almost everyone has had a personal experience with trust being violated and causing pain. It doesn't take many of these incidents to cause people to believe that "trust is earned, not given." Having to wait for team mates to prove their trustworthiness slows down the growth of the team.

Ignoring the process in a group discussion will almost always lead to problems. Paying attention to the process will lead you to a deeper understanding of what is actually happening in the group.

In a high-performance team, group process is not only noticed, it is a natural topic for discussion. More importantly, there should be a contract to do so, arrived at after discussion of the importance of process to the team's success. When all team members become aware of the underlying process, it becomes obvious that it should be dealt with just like any other observed behavior. Universally, teams that discuss their underlying process until it is no longer under the surface, find themselves more satisfied with working on the team.

Developmental Exercise: Content Vs Process

Seeing and understanding process as it occurs takes some practice. While the best possible situation is having the skill to see both the content of a team's discussion and the processes that are going on simultaneously, practicing both at the same time is somewhat difficult for the newly-aware.

It is a little easier for the team leader to drop out of the conversation for a period of time and just observe. If you get a clear request for information, give it and say no more. Take notes on who is doing what to whom. Focus on the process.

Develop hypotheses on what processes are happening both intentionally and unintentionally. See if you can discern patterns in how subgroups of two or three occur. Write them down. Review these notes after the conclusion of the meeting and retain them for further study.

Be cautious in your use of this information in speaking to the team or to any individual member. You are a novice at collecting this information and may be seeing things incorrectly. It has been my experience that the learning curve is shortest for the observer with the most patience. As you feel that you are becoming more accurate in your process detection, you can cautiously start to use the information.

Use of process by the leader

Once you start analyzing the process of what is going on, you will never see your work team as you did before you learned this concept. You will be perpetually aware of the duality of content and process in every meeting, every discussion and every interaction you have. Because both the content and the process are present, it should be obvious that being aware of both is better than being aware of only one. Again, ignorance is not bliss.

The team leader is most effective when understanding is highest. Being aware of both the content and the process will increase your understanding of what the team is doing. As your skills increase in recognizing the team process, you can begin to see patterns of repeated processes. Some of these will be positive. Some will not.

When the team intentionally or unintentionally makes a decision or accomplishes a task without any process problems, take the time to comment on it. It is a behavior that you would like to be repeated, so it needs to be rewarded.

When a team improves its process intentionally, after having seen that previously their process has not been optimal, then you should comment on that even more strongly. It needs to be rewarded even more, because it is a sign of growth and maturity on the part of the team. The more it is rewarded, the more likely it will become an integral part of the way the team operates.

If you notice patterns of behavior on the part of the team that you think might be dysfunctional, make note of them. Changing these patterns should be done, but take considerable thought to do it well. We will discuss this further in the section on GUIDING the team.

Phillip E. Rosner, Ph.D.

Secret 3. Multiple Levels of Behavior

It should be clear by now that there is a lot going on when people assemble in groups and interact. To better understand and observe what is happening, we need to discuss the fact that there are Multiple Levels of Behavior occurring simultaneously. While there are numerous ways to parse these levels, the three that are most productive to be aware of are:

- Individual level
- Small Group Interaction level
- Total Group level

Although these behaviors occur at the same time, for purposes of understanding them, let's look at them one at a time.

Individual Level

Every individual in a group participates in the group discussions. Even if they never say anything, they are a presence in the room.

If you have difficulty understanding this point, try saying absolutely nothing during a committee meeting or in a family discussion. It will not take long before someone says, "Do you have something to say?" or "Is something wrong?" For all intents and purposes, you cannot disappear.

Each individual hears and sees things. Each of these things tends to have some impact on them -- it causes them to think something or feel something. These thoughts and feelings are *hidden from the group* unless the individual chooses to share them. In less mature groups, unless these feelings are quite strong, like love or hate, they tend to remain unspoken. The same is true for whatever thoughts arise in response to what the member hears or sees.

It is also possible that they also may remain *hidden from the individual*. This is true in the sense that thoughts and feelings (especially the latter) are often felt at a non-conscious level. Other members may be able to perceive changes in the member's behavior (e.g. – posture and other body cues, facial expression, type of or lack of participation). Unless these responses are shared with the individual, it might be a long time before the member is even aware of these thoughts and feelings.

The Individual Level, therefore, consists of the unexpressed experience of the individual and the unexpressed perception of that individual by others. It is an internal process to each person, until they express it to others. When that happens, it is transformed into the next level.

Small Group Interactions Level (2 or 3 People)

Some small group interactions (dyads, triads) are easy to see. If two people are directly conversing with each other, that is a small group interaction. You should be paying attention to it and trying to understand what is happening (Content vs. Process), but don't miss the interaction between the dyad and the silent remainder of the group. That, too, is an interaction.

A small group of engineers periodically assembled to find ways to reduce expenditures in order to relieve a budget overrun, Bill and Bob would repeatedly find themselves on opposite sides of most issues. It was clear to everyone that they had some kind of continuous conflict going on, but what wasn't clear to group members was that the overall effect on the group was negative. Every time one of these conflicts would begin, there followed an immediate silence which would remain until their interaction was completed. Even then, it would take a noticeable amount of time before the conversation would resume in any meaningful way.

As the group matured and was able to discuss these interactions, it became obvious that Bill and Bob both were vying for leadership in the group. That would have been a normal function in the group's life, but this was different. It turned out that Bill harbored a resentment against Bob for an incident that occurred several years ago -- of which Bob was unaware!

How could he have known? Bill never told him about it -- it was never discussed -- it just festered inside Bill over the years. Every time they worked together, this resentment had a negative impact on the group and cost them and their company a considerable amount of money due to decreased productivity.

The various people that served on work teams with them knew that something was going on, but the issue was never addressed. Even though the work team was obviously hindered to some degree by their relationship, it was not considered appropriate to address such issues in in the group during work sessions. But not addressing this issue was a mistake.

In decision-making groups, multiple small groups form and disband with ease. Part of the influencing process is to convince people of the correctness of one's position and try to get them to agree. This is normal. It is relatively easy to understand that people interacting in twos and threes are observably behaving at the small group level.

As the team leader learns to see these various simultaneous levels of behavior, a clearer picture of what is happening in the group gradually emerges. As that picture clarifies, the team leader can make better decisions about prioritizing the changes that the team needs to attempt.

Example 1: Giving and Receiving Feedback

The single most important interaction on the Small Group Interaction Level is giving and receiving feedback. It is a skill that is difficult to learn and must be practiced to do well. Yet it takes almost a written contract to get groups to do this effectively. It violates many of the social protocols that many people been taught since childhood. For example: "If you haven't been asked to comment about someone -- keep silent." This concept has, unfortunately, evolved into, "Keep silent even if asked. We don't want to hurt anyone's feelings."

In a working group, everyone has an opinion about how every other member appears to them. These opinions occur spontaneously and with minimal effort. At the same time, each group member has an image about how they think that they come across to others. Although the perfect situation is when these two views are identical, it rarely happens that way.

Group members intentionally keep this valuable information to themselves most of the time. Think about how valuable it would be to you if you knew exactly how you came across to every member of the team. Think about what you could do, in terms of self-improvement, if you knew that information. Think about how much better your work team meetings would be if every member of the group knew exactly how he/she appeared to the other members.

As trust develops in teams, people can become more open to discovering how they come across to others. The act of looking directly at a fellow team member and saying, "I see you as this kind of person who..." gives you a plethora of information. It provides you with an opportunity to interact with that person and do something about the way that they see you. You can be happy about how you are seen and change nothing, or you can be troubled about how you are perceived and try to change the way you come across to that person.

Example 2: Group discussion →→ Small group discussion

A frequent phenomenon in all working groups occurs when a discussion is happening about a topic with multiple alternatives. After a relatively short period, 2 or 3 of these alternatives seem to be the most plausible, and the discussion tends to move to these options (with other alternatives excluded). This is a normal and healthy function of decision-making groups.

Even though, everyone in the group will be affected by the decision, it often occurs that the 2 or 3 alternatives seem to be championed by a single person each. The other members of the group go silent and let the defenders of each position debate each other. It looks like this:

Although no one actually moves their chairs, the discussion proceeds as if there were 2 or 3 chairs in the center of the room and all the other team members are sitting in a circle around the combatants and watching the action. The people in the outer circle are beyond the fray and relatively safe while the people inside the circle do battle on the issue. It is not unusual for the "outside" group to later comment on the discussion of the "inside" group. This happens with considerable frequency and is normal, especially if two or three people are particularly invested in the discussion and the others have no strong feelings about it.

Group Level of Behavior

Groups do things -- as groups -- *independent of what their members do!* We have already mentioned one -- tacit collusion: an unspoken agreement by the group to behave in a certain way. There are lots of these in human society: Most are relatively harmless.

When you are in a new group's first meeting, no formal resolution has to be passed for the group to be polite to each other. There is no vote to speak one-at-a-time or to avoid interrupting each other. Instead, these behaviors are perceived as cultural conventions. You think of people who violate them as being rude but usually say nothing about it -- unless it becomes habitual or annoying.

Groups can also tacitly collude to avoid facing uncomfortable issues.

A senior management team in a large manufacturing operation was having difficulty meeting deadlines. The president asked me to sit in as a non-participant observer on several of their meetings to see if I observed any problems.

I was surprised at how well-organized the team seemed to be: specifying tasks, assigning responsibility for these tasks, and setting up monitoring methods. The only behavior I noticed that was a bit out of place was the assigning an extra person to monitor assignments given to the VP of Sales.

At later meetings, the reason became obvious – the VP of Sales often missed targets, and the second monitor's job was to catch it when it happened. Because the group did not know how to handle internal problems, nothing was said -- they just had someone looking over the VP's shoulder.

When I told the President that he may be faced with a membership issue -- someone who wasn't acting like a functioning member of the group, he denied the accuracy of my observation. Nevertheless, he agreed to have a talk with the VP of Sales. During the talk, the VP admitted that he had been considering an offer from another company and had just decided to accept it –and therefore was leaving the team.

The crisis for the team had been delayed, not averted. They found an unspoken way to adjust to the unreliable nature of the group member. As a group, they did not know why the VP had become unreliable, and they never discussed it with him. They merely adjusted their procedures to work around the problem -- and avoided an uncomfortable discussion.

Parenthetically, the avoidance of the problem had two side effects: First it made the group less efficient, but secondarily, it made the VP of Sales feel less a part of the group. In my opinion, dealing with the problem might have helped the VP to feel like he was more a part of the group and that they cared about what was happening in his life. Perhaps this would have made him less likely to look elsewhere for a place to work.

Tacit collusion is one of the most common mechanisms for groups acting at an unspoken level. It amazes most new process observers how easily a group colludes to avoid doing things that are hard to do, or that are uncomfortable for them. Since it is a group coping mechanism, just like an individual uses subconscious coping mechanisms, it seems natural that groups do this without formal communication.

Groupthink: A Group Level behavior with Negative Consequences

Groupthink is a psychological phenomenon which occurs primarily in decision-making groups. The group acts as if it is seeking uniformity, loyalty, and unanimity. It acts as if it wants to deny the existence of any negativity in the group and enjoy coming to agreed-upon decisions. But this desire for harmony and unity can result in dysfunctional and irrational decisions.

Often there is a tendency to make decisions with incomplete or inaccurate information. People with contradictory information or different opinions tend to stifle their expression in order to foster a pleasant atmosphere and avoid controversy. Raising opposing alternatives or viewpoints is seen as disloyalty to the group and discouraged. The result is minimizing the degree of critical thinking and a lack of realistic outcome-testing.

The most commonly referenced example of this phenomenon is the decision to invade Cuba by the John F. Kennedy Administration. That decision was made by extremely intelligent and experienced individuals and was a disaster from the very beginning. Looking back on the decision-making process, all participants agreed that reality-testing was not much in evidence. They needed a solution to a problem and they misperceived the negative side of the reality of the situation in order to find one.

Developmental Exercise: Multiple Levels of Behavior

As with the last exercise, the best way of developing the ability to see this part of team behavior is to look for it. It is best done initially with the same procedure recommended previously. Intentionally ask yourself, "What is happening at the individual, small group and whole group levels?" Record your observations on paper. You will get better at seeing multiple levels over time.

Try to focus on what the group as a whole is doing. At first, you should be able to see these things after the fact. As you get better at observing them, you will start to notice when the group starts doing group level things.

Most people report that they have some difficulty seeing group level behavior as it is happening. If that is the case, take process notes and consider group level activities after the meeting is concluded. It is easier to see these effects "in the rear-view mirror." The more you recognize them, the easier it will be to see the next ones. This is true at all three levels.

Use of Multiple Levels by the Leader

Ultimately, as the team leader, you will be trying to understand what is happening in the team in order to better make decisions about how to direct them. Since things are happening at all three levels at the same time, recognizing what is happening at each level will allow you to better evaluate what needs to change.

This happens in two different ways. First, you will be able to understand more of the things that need to change. Often, especially in the early stages of team development, all three levels need to improve. Second, you will become better able to evaluate the importance of each level's need for change and make decisions about which changes to prioritize.

Team development professionals typically "staff" each team session. They basically get together and compare notes on what has happened and which changes are needed by the team and by each team member. This allows them to be on the lookout for opportunities to make those changes in a natural manner, rather than artificially telling each person what changes they need to make in a change session.

As the team's leader, you will naturally look at the group's progress toward achieving their assigned tasks. In addition, you can "staff" the meeting by yourself in terms of which directions you want to move the team's growth as a team. You can also think about how individual members' effectiveness and participation level can be improved in the way they work with others in the team. This internal staffing allows you to develop informal plans for how to improve the way the group and its individual members perform.

Chapter Summary

Leadership INSIGHT grows exponentially by the use of these three secrets:

- Understanding the Law of Reinforcement and how to use it to recognize rewards and punishments dispensed by the team and its members
- Knowing the existence of both Content and Process and its significance to team outcomes allows you to see more of what is happening as your team works, and
- Recognizing that team behavior occurs at multiple levels simultaneously will increase your understanding of its complexity

The three secrets discussed in this chapter will increase your ability to see what is actually happening. No matter what your leadership style or your belief in any particular leadership philosophy, you can't affect a problem if you do not see it happening. Once you see the dysfunction of the group, you cannot ignore it. You will feel a compulsion to influence the problem until you no longer see it. It is your choice as to which type of management style or philosophy you apply to fix the problem.

Becoming aware of how your team is functioning is the next step in developing Leadership INSIGHT. The above three concepts will help you get a better picture of the team itself. Now it is time to recognize the human behavior of the team members.

As members of the human race, there are some commonalities that appear when people interact in groups. We next look at a pair of characteristics that have a considerable impact on group functioning and eventual group effectiveness.

Chapter FOUR
Understanding People

Most people know that psychology is the study of behavior. Whether that behavior is performed by people or animals, individually or in groups, by societies or organizations, the focus is on observable behavior. In general, psychologists try to understand behavior and ultimately hope to predict it.

In the practical world of work teams, you try to understand what the behavior you observe means. You ask questions like: Why did that behavior show up in our last meeting? Is that normal (whatever "normal" exactly means)? Answering the question, "Why did he/she/they do that?" is the essential question for developing insight into people.

The next two secrets are designed to help you develop Leadership INSIGHT by increasing your knowledge of how to understand people. You cannot read minds, but you can develop an understanding of the behavior you see. This is true for people in general, but is especially true for those people in your work teams and the behavior you observe during team deliberations.

Secret 4, "Thoughts versus Feelings", is a distinction that is critical in listening to what your team mates are actually saying. Many people use the terms "thoughts" and "feelings" interchangeably – but they are not interchangeable! The two words have different meanings and convey different messages. They also have different impacts on the team discussion.

The differences between thoughts and feelings are made clear in this chapter. It is a critical distinction that must be made if you, as the team leader, are able to target change strategies correctly. It takes some practice differentiating between the two because team members often mislabel them.

Secret 5, Internal vs. External "Locus of Control" (LOC), is a description of the degree to which a person believes that he/she controls what happens to them. It is a continuum describing whether they see these outcomes as being of their own doing or as the result of external forces beyond their control. It is one of the basic ways people view what happens to them in life.

Because it involves their perception of the world and its impact on them, Locus of Control also has a major impact on what they consequently do when the need for corrective action arises. It can be a major factor in how the person responds to the world. For the team leader, it may point the way toward how to change that individual's typical behavior.

LOC is one of the strongest factors in personal and team development. Like other psychological traits, it is a tendency to behave in a certain manner. Also, like other psychological traits, it is difficult to change. However, knowledge of LOC and understanding how it affects people will allow the team leader to interact with the person more effectively.

Secret 4. Thoughts versus feelings

In everyday conversation, as mentioned, people tend to misuse the terms "Thoughts" and "Feelings." Yet the difference between the two is considerable. Thoughts are just what you think they are -- that little voice in your head that talks to you. "XYZ would solve this problem if applied this way". "I wonder if ABC would work to solve this problem."

You may be aware of your thinking while it is happening. Most people often pose questions to themselves and begin an internal dialog. Thoughts mostly take place only in the brain and many are not expressed. Much of the time, you can assert conscious control over your thoughts. If you don't like the flow of thoughts in your head, you can change it by starting to think about something else or by internally singing a song to distract yourself.

Feelings, on the other hand, are not within our ability to control. They are recognized or acknowledged by the brain, but are not controlled by it. However, you do have considerable ability to control whether these feelings are apparent to others. Many people expend a great deal of mental and physical energy on keeping their feelings secret.

Some people find it more effective to use the term, "Feelings are..." They just happen. In reality, feelings are skeletal in nature, like reflexes -- that is, they occur in those parts of your nervous system (mid-and lower-brain, as well as peripheral nerves) that are automatic.

If someone insults you, your body senses it immediately. Some people call it a gut reaction. It doesn't require much thought to experience it. Your body reacts automatically -- your face may flush, your heart rate increases, your palms may sweat, etc. At that point, your conscious brain may kick in, and you can start thinking about the feeling (ignoring it, rationalizing its truth, actually accepting it as truth). But thinking about a feeling is objectively and subjectively different from feeling it.

How Feelings Look in a Work Team

"Don't bring feelings into the office." That expression is equivalent to Tom Hanks' saying, "There's no crying in baseball" in the movie "A League of Their Own." On the surface, it seems to make sense, but when you think about it, it is actually non-sense. Feelings are part of you. How could you not bring them wherever you go? What the expression REALLY means is: "Don't let your feelings *show* in the office."

Psychologists know that the continuous suppression of one's feelings has highly negative consequences. On the other hand, constantly dealing with your world only in terms of your own feelings can be equally negative. Learning to deal appropriately with one's feelings in the office is the goal.

When the word, "that" follows the words, "I feel," very often a misstatement is about to be uttered. "I feel that ..." is another way of saying "I think that ...". People use that phrase when they are unsure of what they are saying, as in "I feel that we should do such and such..." or "I feel that this will not work".

"I feel..." should always be followed by some kind of expression of feeling (or a reflection of that feeling)."I feel good" is NOT a feeling. It is the evaluation of a set of feelings that might include calmness, satisfaction, a slow breathing rate and heartbeat, satisfaction from removing a stressor, etc. "I feel bad" is also NOT a feeling. It might be the evaluation of a set of feelings that could include, rapid breathing, nervousness, nausea or other queasiness, fear, etc.

The more mature the team, the more intimate the feelings that can be expressed. It is quite common for mature teams to hear things like, "I am uncomfortable about what is happening now. I don't know exactly what is wrong, but I am starting to feel scared. Maybe we are going in the wrong direction." Mature teams have learned to value vague reports of "bodily reactions" to what is happening and can take the time to explore what might be causing it. Since we can't control what our body tells us, sometimes it is more sensitive to what is happening than our brains.

The difference between thoughts and feelings would be relatively unimportant if thoughts and feelings were equal. They are NOT!

Thoughts and feelings happen all the time, but most people are more aware of their thoughts because "that little voice in our heads" is something we listen to. It helps us figure things out and make sense of our world.

The feelings are there too. However, for most people, they have to reach a stronger level to be noticed. Most of the time, you probably don't really notice when you are a little happy or a little sad. Most people tend to live more in their thoughts rather than their feelings. But if a friend calls you "stupid" or you discover that you were not invited to a party you wanted to attend, watch the intensity shoot up. This applies to positive emotions also. If your boss walks up to you and says, "You did a GREAT job on that last presentation," or someone you care about says, "I am so glad that you are in my life," your entire body will react.

To the extent that you get better at recognizing your thoughts and feelings, this knowledge can help you deal with your work teams. This is because many people give a higher value to their emotions than to their thoughts. If a team member tells us you he disagrees with an item, you probably take note of it. If he starts crying (or yelling) when saying it, your ears will perk up. Whether this happens for most people because they want to avoid emotions, because they are sensitive to them or because they are seen as signals for concern, they pay more attention.

Recognition of feelings is a useful tool that needs sharpening.

Imagine how convenient it would be to have an invisible lie detector at every meeting. You would know whether what you are hearing is true or false. In a sense, you actually have one, and you have probably already used it.

> *Most people have experienced a situation in which they are talking with someone, and an internal voice starts to tell them that what they are hearing is not true. It is a sort of "bull-pucky" detector. You don't have any consciously clear evidence of any misstatements, but you know that what you are hearing is false. You haven't heard a fact that you know is untrue, but your guard is going up. Much of the time, this vague warning proves to be correct. That's why you pay attention to the signal. You may not be conscious of why it's there, but experience has proven its reliability and accuracy.*

Psychologists and other professionals who often deal with people in stressful situations are taught to listen to this lie detector and to consciously sharpen it as a tool. It doesn't provide answers to specific questions, but it allows the pursuit of answers by the professional. It signals that something is not right and that a more in-depth exploration may be needed. It enables the development of insight into other people.

Team leaders can use this tool in much the same way. The signal that something is wrong about a situation is the starting point from which to begin an exploration of what is causing the signal to be sent. It may not be 100 percent accurate, but it causes the leader to be more cautious about accepting everything that is said.

Additionally, this personal lie detector has two other advantages: 1) It is free. You didn't have to go to the electronics store to buy it. 2) It sends its signals silently so the other person doesn't know it was set off. If it turns out to be wrong – no harm, no foul.

Developmental Exercise:

Take note of whenever you get this "something is wrong" signal. Enter it in your process notes. Either during the meeting or after, try to figure out: 1) Was it accurate? and 2) What caused the signal to be generated? Don't be discouraged if you have difficulty doing this. It takes time and effort to sharpen this skill into a consistently useful tool.

Use of Thinking vs. Feelings by the Team Leader

The team leader needs to learn how their team members use the words "think" and "feel." Even when used correctly, they can have different shades of meaning. "I think that…" may be a weaker statement than a simple declarative sentence. "I feel that…" may be even weaker.

The use or misuse of these words may illustrate something about power relationships in your team. A team member quickly learns that some other members may see a declarative sentence as a direct challenge. Using "I feel that…" may be seen as less of a challenge.

It is critical to note how your team members deal with each other. With prolonged and meticulous observation, language use between members can be used to discover a pecking order within the group. Understanding how your people deal with each other when engaged in important discussions can tell you what things need to be changed.

As the team leader, you want the individuals on your team to feel comfortable in discussing things among themselves with no trepidation. All team members may not be equal in their technical knowledge and experience, but they should feel equally free to express themselves.

Secret 5. Internal vs. External Locus of Control (LOC)

When trying to understand other people, whether it's in the workplace or elsewhere, it is important to have an understanding of the major filters that people use to interpret their world. People develop these filters sometimes consciously, sometimes not. They contribute to personality, but are somewhat different.

These filters are more like typical ways of behaving due to the different ways people perceive the world and their place in it. Most people know about the most common typical ways of behaving, like being:

- Shy or outgoing
- Quiet or loud
- Introverted or extroverted
- More intellectual or more emotional.

A better understanding of the people you hire and work with is a good thing. While psychologists and business leaders have developed a basic understanding of the behavior associated with various personality types in the workplace, there is one that I and many psychologists have found particularly useful in understanding ones team mates and their behavior in the workings of the team.

Much of what we do in our lives depends on how we see and interpret what happens. In the mid-20th century, psychologist Julian B. Rotter (1956) postulated the concept of a personality aspect which he named: Internal vs. External Locus of Control (LOC). His theory postulates that people differ in how they view things that affect their lives. It also involves the issue of control. There is basically a continuum that runs from Internal LOC to External LOC.

At one end of this continuum, a person with a primarily External LOC, tends to believe that much of what happens to them is beyond their control -- it is caused by influences that are external to them. The important consideration can be stated as, "If the causes of my success or failure are external to me and beyond my control, there is little I can do about it."

At the other end, a person with a primarily Internal LOC tends to believe that the control of much of their lives and their successes or failures directly results from actions that they manage. The important consideration can be stated as, "Since I control what happens to me, I must always try to discover what I did (or didn't do) that resulted in the outcome."

> A typical example is the salesperson who fails to make the sale and asks himself, "Why did I not get the sale?" The external LOC person thinks, "Our price was too high, or our reputation is not good, or the customer was in a bad mood, or it's raining outside, or it was God's will." The critical and most salient point is that after this train of thought, the salesperson with an external LOC does not accept personal responsibility for the lost sale. In addition, since he believes that he can't do anything about any of these things, there is nothing he needs to do before his next sales call. He didn't cause the lost sale, so he can walk into the next potential customer's office without having to change his approach.

> In contrast, the internal LOC person thinks, "I should have said this, or I should have done that, or I could have prepared better, etc." Here the salient point is that the internal LOC person is looking for things that can be changed to improve the probability of being successful on the next call. His approach to the situation causes him to look for behavior changes that may improve the results in the future.

Some people can keep both approaches in their heads at the same time. In the first example, if the sale is not made, the answer to "Why?" could be those listed above. However, if the same external LOC sales person makes the sale, the answer to "Why?" is typically something akin to: "Because I am a great salesperson, or because I won't take no for an answer, or because I ..." In other words, "It's ME (internal LOC) when I succeed and it's OUTSIDE FORCES (external LOC) when I fail".

There are sales managers who believe that having both Internal and External LOC approaches available when convenient helps the salesperson get psychologically ready for the next call. In my experience, I have found many non-sales professionals (doctors, lawyers, engineers, accountants, etc.) who find it very difficult to make another call after a failure experience. They tend to focus on what *they* did wrong and get personally involved in their shortcomings to the point where the next call is almost unbearable.

In general, the business world tends to reward people with an Internal LOC. This is because most personal development comes from observing your behavior, deciding whether other behaviors might better serve you, deciding to try out other behaviors and lots of practice. The internal LOC person, by definition, is looking for things she should change. In contrast, the person with an External LOC believes that things just happen to her, and she has little control over her life. The business world is less likely to reward the person with an External LOC.

Developmental Exercise: Where is my LOC?

In 1966, J. B. Rotter published a scale to measure a person's Locus of Control. The Scale and its scoring key are presented below. I have included it to give you an idea of where you stand as the team leader. Before you take the instrument, ask yourself, "Where will I score on the internal vs. external continuum?" Answer the 13 questions as honestly as you can. Obviously faking the test by answering the questions in the way you think that you should will not benefit you. Think about each question and select the choice that fits you better than the other choice. It's a "more or less" choice, not a "perfect fit" choice.

Rotter's Locus of Control Scale

For each question, select the statement that you agree with most. You may disagree with them both, but choose the one that is closer to what you think.

1. a. Many of the unhappy things in people's lives are partly due to bad luck.
   b. People's misfortunes result from the mistakes they make.

2. a. One of the major reasons why we have wars is because people don't take enough interest in politics.
   b. There will always be wars, no matter how hard people try to prevent them.

3. a. In the long run: people get the respect they deserve in this world.
   b. Unfortunately, an individual's worth often passes unrecognized no matter how hard he tries.

4. a. The idea that teachers are unfair to students is nonsense.
   b. Most students don't realize the extent to which their grades are influenced by accidental happenings.

5. a. Without the right breaks, one cannot be an effective leader.
    b. Capable people who fail to become leaders have not taken advantage of their opportunities.

6. a. No matter how hard you try, some people just don't like you.
    b. People who can't get others to like them don't understand how to get along with others.

7. a. I have often found that what is going to happen will happen.
    b. Trusting to fate has never turned out as well for me as making a decision to take a definite course of action.

8. a. In the case of the well prepared student, there is rarely, if ever, such a thing as an unfair test.
    b. Many times exam questions tend to be so unrelated to course work that studying is really useless.

9. a. Becoming a success is a matter of hard work; luck has little or nothing to do with it.
    b. Getting a good job depends mainly on being in the right place at the right time.

10. a. The average citizen can have an influence in government decisions.
    b. This world is run by the few people in power, and there is not much the little guy can do about it.

11. a. When I make plans, I am almost certain that I can make them work.

 b. It is not always wise to plan too far ahead because many things turn out to be a matter of luck anyway.

12. a. In my case, getting what I want has little or nothing to do with luck.

 b. Many times we might just as well decide what to do by flipping a coin.

13. a. What happens to me is my own doing.

 b. Sometimes I feel that I don't have enough control over the direction my life is taking.

Score one point for each of the following:

1. a, 2. a, 3. a, 4. a, 5. b, 6. a, 7.a, 8. b, 9. b, 10. b, 11. b, 12. b, 13. b.

This test was designed to be somewhat vague in that it only gives an indication of where you might fit on the scale. It was never intended to give you an exact score as does an IQ test. It does not tell you that a score between x and y has a specific meaning. The closer you are to the ends of the scale, the more internally or externally you view your world. It is the general concept that is useful.

A higher score = External Locus of Control
A lower score = Internal Locus of Control

Now that you have scored your test, how happy are you with the result? Did you accurately guess where you fit on the scale? Does your internal or external LOC serve you well? If your answers are mostly "Yes", Great! If your answers are mostly "No", try to listen to yourself when you think about your successes and failures. Are you hearing words that will lead you to improving your performance or are you hearing words that excuse your shortcomings? Try to practice saying to yourself, "What could I have done to improve my performance?" Changing your LOC takes time and desire, but it can be done.

How to use the concept of LOC as a team leader

Take a good look at the past behavior of your work team. Try to see how each of them would rate on the External to Internal LOC test.

Remember – You are NOT a psychologist and you have not been asked to help another person change any aspect of his personality! That does not mean that you can't help your team member to improve his performance on the team. So – first try to assess whether their LOC is causing them problems and whether they are aware of it. If that behavior enables them to avoid fixing problems, think about talking to them about it. Do so gingerly!

If you think it might be helpful, take the time to encourage those with an external Locus of Control to try to find more things that they can control to improve their performance. Just because a person is externally locus-oriented, it doesn't mean that they have lost the ability to see the relationship between behavior change and performance improvement.

Is There a Team Locus of Control?

There is no team locus of control. But in one sense, the actions of the team should reflect an internal Locus of Control. Regardless of any individual's LOC orientation, it is part of the team leader's job to help the team maximize its performance. As leader, you can help the team to habitually look for things they can do to improve the team's performance. Obviously, if the team is excusing failure to perform with an "external LOC-type excuse", insist that they overlook that idea and search harder for things that can be corrected or improved.

Chapter Summary

Obviously, understanding people is not limited to the two concepts presented in this chapter. I have selected to discuss Thoughts vs. Feelings and Locus of Control because they often affect team functioning, and they have an important effect on team behavior and effectiveness.

It takes many sessions of team building before one sees the gradual disappearance of the phrase "I feel that ..." This is true even if it is corrected the first time it appears and is discourage whenever it reappears.

When the individual team members start to look at their feelings during work discussions as clues to how they are responding to the content, they start seeing more of the complexities of that discussion. Feeling good about the outcome of a decision-making session is a stronger positive sign than merely thinking that the decision is good.

Locus of Control is often seen as a personality trait more than a set of habitual behaviors. I disagree with such a characterization. With the help of a well-functioning team, I have seen individuals successfully reverse their LOC from external to internal. While most personality traits can be changed with considerable effort, I believe that LOC is a bit easier to change.

As a team leader, understanding the members of your team as people rather than as personnel that carry out work functions, allows you to have many more options in helping them to become more effective as team members and as people.

Chapter FIVE
Understanding Teams

Most people have heard the expression: "The whole is greater than the sum of its parts." That is a truth. It is often referred to as "synergy" and is frequently represented by the formula:

$$1 + 1 = 3$$

In addition, when referring to teams in the workplace, one often hears the expression: "The team is more than the sum of its members". In the previous discussion of multiple levels of group interaction it was pointed out that the team, independently of its individual members, at times, acts as a unit.

In order to develop and sharpen one's Leadership INSIGHT, it is important to know that well-functioning teams have certain tendencies. They are really cultural approaches to the workplace specifically and to the world in general. They are reflections of the ways people look at the work world when they operate in teams.

They exist because, in general, teams are formed by people of good will who want to succeed at their jobs. They understand that if the team does not succeed at accomplishing its assigned tasks, then their jobs (and indeed the entire enterprise) are placed in jeopardy.

Leadership INSIGHT is enhanced by being aware of these tendencies. They tend to form a normative standard by which to judge the workings of the team. When the team is acting in ways that are contrary to these tendencies, this knowledge provides a signal that something is wrong. It may not provide a crystal clear idea of how to correct the team, but it will signal that the leader (and the team members) should be looking for the source of the problem and searching for a method of correction.

Secret 6. Teams Desire Democratic Values

In the first half of the 20th Century, authoritarian management was the style of choice in the business world. There was a boss and there were subordinates. The boss made the decisions and the subordinates carried them out. That system was relatively effective in small low-tech organizations. The boss was an expert in the technical aspects of the entire process and, in effect, monitored, and assisted in all aspects of the work.

As the world became more complicated and more technically oriented, the boss could no longer continue to be an expert in all the necessary sub-fields of the industry. Teams evolved to be led by a manager of specialists. The specialists were expected to keep abreast of new developments in their respective fields. The manager could not be expected to keep pace in all of these fields. This resulted in a situation in which the manager had to know enough technically about each specialty to manage each specialist, but they all knew their specialties better than the boss.

As the 20th century moved toward its end, managers found that authoritarian management styles were causing employee dissatisfaction and were less effective. This was not an easy transition for a lot of managers. In some places, it is still not an easy transformation for some companies.

An International Example:

I was asked by the American division of a German company to help with multiple dysfunctional teams. I designed a team-development program to help several of their teams to work together more effectively.

The fact that each team had Germans from the parent company made the program both more interesting and somewhat different. The German team members had never been exposed to non-authoritarian team leadership. The Germans were used to a highly authoritarian management style, but they truly enjoyed the more democratic style of their high-performance teams.

During the course of the program they told me about the "Vier-Augen Prinzip" (the Four-Eyes Principle) utilized by the parent company. According to this principle, whenever authority was delegated, TWO monitors of the decision were employed to assure the quality of the decision and to avoid negligence or misdeeds. This intentional open act of distrust by the company caused people to be suspicious of their fellow team members. Overcoming this management principle among the German members took a while to accomplish.

Two months after the program, I received a call from the parent company in Germany congratulating the success of my program with all of the teams and commenting about the obvious increase in productivity. They told me that the reports from the German members of the new teams were both glowing and unexpected. Furthermore, they invited me to design a corporate-wide set of team development programs to be used throughout the company (mostly in Germany).

I told them that I would be glad to design and carry out such a program, but that it would not work unless the company would formally abandon the Vier-Augen Prinzip. I explained how important trust was in the process and that it could not succeed under that management style.

Several weeks later, the company president called to tell me that: 1) he and his staff had spoken to several other professionals about doing team-building and basically received the same message from them, and 2) while they understood the need to build trust in their company, they could NOT abandon their current management style. He explained that such a style was ingrained in their culture and that, while the employees might prefer a more democratic style, the senior managers would not tolerate it.

Teams reflect their underlying values

The underlying values of high-performance team functioning are the same as those for democracy: Equality, Free Speech and Good Citizenship. Severely limit any one of these and it becomes difficult for the team to function at peak efficiency. One of the leader's jobs is to monitor the behavior of the team to make sure that these values are continuously practiced.

Equality

In high-performance teams, all people are equal when discussing issues. Of course, there are people with more important titles, different levels of power, and (most importantly) more expertise. There is an appreciation for and a general acceptance of the idea that everyone has the right to speak and contribute to the debate. Dissenters are especially valued. They keep the group honest. If the decision is time-limited, the team leader will have the responsibility to get the decision made in a timely manner. However, that leader is well aware that a forced decision is less likely to be successful.

Free Speech

There is a very strong correlation between the quality of a work team and the presence of freedom of speech within the team. When people feel that they can speak freely, can make mistakes, can say potentially dumb things, and can propose unusual solutions, the exchange of ideas will be more fruitful. Free speech is freedom from social risk. Most of us have experienced this among friends. If something dumb is said, everyone laughs -- they don't deride the speaker and threaten his/her career. This free and friendly atmosphere is the best in which to find solutions to problems. Limitation of free speech results in limited numbers of and poorer quality of ideas.

Good Citizenship

It is also the obligation of each member to step up from time to time and take the role for which they are best suited. If the discussion revolves around your particular expertise, you probably should assume some of the leadership of the discussion. No law requires you to do so -- you do it because it is right for the progress of the team. The team accepts that leadership because it makes sense. No one nominates you, you just do it.

Similarly, if one or more members recognize an underlying process happening that seems to be hindering the team's progress, they have both the right and the obligation to bring it up. This recognition that the quality of functioning of the team is of a higher priority at the moment than the actual decision being made is one of the key characteristics of a high-performance team. There is an appreciation of the notion that ignoring the underlying process hurts the team both short-term and long-term.

The Use of Democratic Values as the Team Leader

The least effective way to insure that democratic values are promoted in your work team is to tell them about it. Lectures are intended for times when the leader perceives a lack of information on the part of the team. A prolonged set of statements in this area is likely to be received with a sigh and a "we already know that" attitude.

An acceptable second choice would be a review of a set of behavioral events (illustrating the lack of democratic functioning) that just occurred in the team's work process. It could be followed by a discussion of how what happened did not work well and what might be substituted in its place.

The best teaching method for the team leader is definitely modeling those democratic values. If the team leader acts in a consistent way that demonstrates his view of each member as equal, encourages free speech, and displays actions that show that he/she is a good citizen, the message will most likely be clearly received without discussion. At worst, it might naturally stimulate such a discussion.

Be cautious about the role you play. Pay attention to how the group is behaving. When you sense some signs of non-equality, restriction of freedom and poor citizenship you should consider doing something about it. At the first sign of these, DO NOT jump in (unless the behavior is extreme). See if the group will do something about it naturally. Allow the group to do this self-correction in a democratic way. The critical idea is that democratic values are the desired norm. Deviation indicates a need to do something about it, (Interventions is discussed fully in Chapter 6.)

Phillip E. Rosner, Ph.D.

Secret 7. An Innate Sense of Right and Wrong

There is an innate sense of right and wrong which shows up when healthy teams are functioning well. There seem to always be one or more people in the team who consistently and informally monitor the team for unethical behavior. They do so as part of their belief that it is one of the natural functions of everyone in the company. Of course, this is done automatically without actually assigning the role to people. If the team starts to head off in an unethical direction while in the process of making decisions, someone will typically point it out. The sign of health is that, when attention is brought to a possibly unethical decision, the team typically modifies it.

This is a phenomenon that I have seen in every team with which I have worked for the past four decades. Contrary to most theorists, who speak about how individual members of groups try to optimize their outcomes as individuals, groups frequently develop a sense of "team-ness" which sets the goals of the group above their own goals. To say this in a technically correct way, the members of the team find a way to align their individual goals with the team's goals in such a way that both cannot be accomplished independently. They need to work together so that both the team's goals and their individual goals can be accomplished.

Super-ordinate goals

This concept of individual members subordinating their personal benefit to the group's needs has a counterpart when two teams interact.   When a group is near the end of a team-building program, they typically demonstrate a phenomenon which was first encountered in Sherif, et al, (1961), typically called "The Robbers' Cave Experiment."

> *Two groups of boys in a summer camp each formed their intra-group attachments while not knowing that the other group existed. When one team accidentally discovered the other, they became quite hostile to each other. The experimenters (acting in the role of camp counsellors) tried many adjustments that failed to remove the hostility.*

> *They eventually discovered that both teams achieved a solid level of cooperation and camaraderie when faced with a situation in which both groups wanted to achieve a desired end, but could not do so unless they cooperated with each other. The experimenters called this end point a "super-ordinate goal" -- a situation in which a desired outcome can only be reached when both groups can only solve the problem working together. When such a situation was given to the boys, they eventually cooperated so they could solve the problem, and in the course of the exercise, they developed a camaraderie.*

The underlying message of such a situation is simply that a group's individual members override their individual or even their sub-team goals when they perceive that the overall group goals will only get accomplished if they work together. This is frequently expressed as "doing what is right." Most group members can easily figure out what is right and what is wrong in a given situation. High performance teams seem to do this consistently with minimal effort.   I have found only one team which apparently did not follow this pattern.

The Contrary Example

I was working with an executive team because they had failed to gel naturally for almost two years. During the course of a four month team development program, a pattern quickly emerged in which the Sales Vice President, Mr. Z, seemed to be consistently (either through direct comments or through his silence) working contrary to the team's best interests.

At first, I thought that he might be unaware of the effects of his actions. As the team progressed, I became certain that Mr. Z knew what he was doing, but I had difficulty figuring out the reason for his behavior. As the group matured in their ability to confront each other productively, one of his teammates brought up the subject, pointing out Mr. Z's comments during the current discussion.

Mr. Z denied the validity of his teammate's observation, and started to spin that observation into an accidental and therefore irrelevant coincidence. One of the other team members said that he remembered another similar incident. Again Mr. Z denied it. I had accumulated a list of several incidences where the same behavior occurred and recited some of them to the team.

When faced with a preponderance of evidence of his unusual behavior, Mr. Z became silent for a minute and then told the team that he had been planning to leave the company for more than a year, and that he was going to work for their largest competitor. The shock of the other team members was palpable. No one knew what to do. The revelation threatened to literally destroy the team.

While this kind of revelation *during* a team building exercise is rare, the feelings engendered were very real. I gently moved the group away from the discussion they were having to a discussion about *membership, loyalty, betrayal,* and perceived *sabotage*. The focus was on how to deal with these feelings and keep the team together. Fortunately, we were in a Leadership Laboratory setting, and could take the time necessary to resolve the issue.

I present this single contrary example because, as the only contrary occurrence during my entire career, it stands out in my mind. There have been hundreds of occasions in which the principle of "team over self" followed true. Here's a more typical example:

At a strategy meeting, an executive team member presented a plan to steal market share from their largest competitor. It involved doing some (in my opinion) mean things to their rival, but nothing illegal or unethical. Worse than that, it seemed like it would have worked.

It seemed likely that following this plan would cause the team's company to gain market share while the rival company would suffer and might be forced out of business. Most likely, the rival company would never have known what had been done to them.

As I was deciding whether or not I should intervene, several members of the team jumped into the discussion with comments that basically told the proposing member that the plan was a terrible idea and was "just plain wrong." They further expressed the notion that the team's job was to increase their share of the market, "not destroy the other company." In a matter of seconds, the team concluded that the plan was "just not right," and rejected it. A new plan was devised and implemented.

While I allow that there may exist company executive teams that pride themselves on being predatory and winning at all costs, and would have happily adopted the above-described strategy, my experience leads me to believe that they are few in number. "Live and let live" seems to be more prevalent than "Win at any price" in the companies to which I have been exposed.

Use of this Innate Sense of Right and Wrong by the team leader

There are basically two ways to use this concept as the team leader. Both ways require a gentle touch.

If the team is, in your opinion, heading off in a poor direction – wait. Remember discussion is generally healthy and should be allowed to continue. Nothing will be decided until there is a call for a show of agreement. Your patience will usually be rewarded by a change in direction because teams tend to do what is right (eventually).

If that doesn't occur without your intervention, the alternative intervention is a simple one. As a member of the group, you always have the right to ask, "Is what we are contemplating as our decision the right and honorable thing to do?" All you are really doing is bringing up the issue. It would have been better if one of the team members had done so, and you doing it does have extra weight because you are the team leader. Nevertheless, as leader, you do not forfeit your membership rights (or obligations) in the team.

When the use of this last question (Is it right?) does not move the group toward a better solution, you, as team leader, have a more difficult task before you. First, you must re-examine yourself and try to determine who is correct, you or the team? Perhaps you are seeing the ethics of the proposed solution incorrectly.

If you are certain that your view of the solution is correct, the new issue is, "Why do they not see that this is wrong?" What is it about your team that keeps them from seeing it? At this point, you must ask yourself who is saying what and how is it being received by the various team members? If the individuals are basically moral people, perhaps they don't understand the kind of people your company is supposed to have. Perhaps a clarification of your mission or vision statements is called for.

Remember to remain calm. Ultimately, you are the final authority and retain all of the responsibility for all decisions made by the team. You can discuss your position, argue your position, cajole them to move toward your position and, if absolutely necessary, veto their decision. A veto is very unlikely to be necessary. Teams usually do what is right.

Chapter Summary

The two concepts discussed in this chapter are universal. Leadership INSIGHT comes from being aware of them and noticing when they are missing or are somehow distorted.

Democratic Values

The desire for democratic values is not limited to those countries which have a democratic political culture. The "Vier Augen Prinzip" came from an autocratic company within a democratic country. In countries which clearly are anti-democratic, there are constant reports of groups trying to be more democratic. In non-capitalistic countries, in which having more resources than your neighbor is seen as improper, people still try to accumulate wealth.

An Innate Sense of Right and Wrong

The importance of teams doing the right thing when allowed to choose for themselves is a reality. That does not mean that a team cannot make selfish or evil choices. It means that, in general, they tend not to do that. I have personally seen many team situations in which the question "Are we doing the right thing?" has reversed a lengthy process of debate and discussion. Perhaps it is the public nature of the team setting that guides teams toward the Good.

It is when the team appears to be heading in a wrong direction that the leader takes notice. Redirecting a team toward the Good typically requires a nudge, not a sledgehammer.

The insightful team leader uses these characteristics of teams to see if the team is moving in the right direction. They are a useful barometer in helping the team leader in deciding what to do. If the team is functioning in a democratic manner, is ethically sound and appears to be improving, the leader knows that he is on the right track.

Chapter SIX
GUIDING the Team using Leadership INSIGHT

The Public Nature of the Team's Interactions

If your goal is to develop your team into a Championship Team (one that is high-performing year after year), you need to establish an understanding with every team member about two things:

First, each team member must have a clear idea of what you are asking them to achieve. They need to know what a high-performance team looks like and how one performs. They cannot commit to a vague notion of better performance or some kind of increased effectiveness. Draw a clear verbal picture for them of how a high-performance team acts and what it is capable of achieving.

Second, each team member needs to commit to public learning, public discussion of their behavior in the team and public behavior change. "Public" in this case refers to information shared only within the team and its members. It does not refer to having that information revealed or discussed outside of team meetings. This is not an effort that can be done effectively in one-on-one conferences with the boss.

Long before I started working in the corporate world, employee improvement was guided by a simple expression, "Reward in public and discipline in private." It seems like a sound principle at first. It avoids any public embarrassment and allows team members to bask in those reward-moments.

It establishes a motivation to receive rewards, but one issue is that it doesn't make clear what is being rewarded. It certainly doesn't allow the other team members to see what behaviors need to be corrected. In addition, team members may be aware of other team members who need correction, but they don't know if the correction has been addressed unless it was made in public.

An atmosphere in which everyone has agreed to improve their behavior and become better, both as people and as team members, is also an atmosphere that decreases the negativity of pointing out the need for more effective functioning. It allows each member to see progress being made and increases the reward value of such improvement. Most importantly, it allows other team members to learn appropriate and more effective behaviors from the mistakes and successes of others. It focuses on the team meeting as the place where rewards for behavior change occur rather than in the team leader's office.

Being a Team Leader not a Manipulator

What is the difference between "leading the team" and "manipulating the team?" In both cases, the leader is trying to get the team to move in some direction. In both cases, the leader is trying to shape the behavior of the team. Yet "leading" is a neutral to a positive term while "manipulating" is clearly pejorative, conjuring up images of a puppet master pulling on the strings.

There are two basic differences between the two terms:

Intention – A manipulation implies that the action is taken to cause the target to go in a direction that they might not choose for themselves. It also implies some level of secrecy or hidden agenda on the part of the leader. It's as if the team is being moved against its will.

Contract – Leadership of a work team implies that the team knows that the role of the leader includes helping them to move toward their stated goals. Most of the time, this contract is understood rather than stated. In most high-performance teams, this contract is discussed and agreed to very early in the life of the team.

So What Does a Team Leader Do?

The leader helps to guide the group toward its goals in the most efficient way possible.

This is more than merely moving them. A good team leader uses both a force and a direction. That means that the leader must have an idea of what outcomes are desired. The leader must also have an idea of the processes needed to achieve those desired outcomes.

It should be noted that in order to lead effectively, the leader must understand that there may be more than one path that can achieve the right outcome. Flexibility to possible paths allows the leader to guide the team without prescribing the particular steps required. Leaders convince the team to follow their lead. How the leader does this in a high-performance team is the subject of this chapter.

- The leader facilitates the work of the team. This requires understanding of how teams function efficiently.
- The leader models appropriate behavior. The saying, "Do what I say, not what I do" has no place in a high-performance team.
- The leader intentionally intervenes in the life of the group to achieve both long- and short-term positive effects. The leader should do so with clear intent and with decisive methods.

These concepts are critical to Leadership INSIGHT but have usually been kept secret. They are rarely taught in Leadership courses. They are relatively easy to understand but difficult to skillfully implement without clear understanding and practice. They are extremely powerful tools.

Phillip E. Rosner, Ph.D.

Secret 8. Facilitation: A Word with TWO Meanings

The most common usage of the term "facilitation" when referring to groups is a set of skills used to make the meeting flow more smoothly and assist with accomplishing a specific purpose. Meeting facilitators provide a valuable service. When dealing with work teams, the term "facilitation" has a significant additional meaning. The team facilitator is charged with helping the team make long-term changes and become a more effective unit. This requires a different set of skills. We will discuss both kinds of facilitation in greater depth in the following sections.

a. Meeting Facilitation

The word "facilitate" means "to make easy." In the most accepted definition, a meeting facilitator *helps the group make decisions* during their meetings *by keeping them focused on how they are making those decisions*. The meeting facilitator avoids being seen as a member of the group, and also avoids directly contributing content to the group discussion. The meeting facilitator typically *leads that particular group meeting, but is never seen as the group's leader.*

Typical meeting facilitator behavior includes:

- Clarifying and summarizing what has happened
- Maximizing participation
- Accomplishing the agenda
- Taking public notes (frequently on flipcharts),
- Keeping track of time.

Typical outcomes include helping the group arrive at meaningful decisions and task solutions, success with a specific achievement or document (e.g. - a succession plan or a business strategy, or a long-term business plan). In addition, the group experiences a more effective group interaction through the example of the facilitator modeling effective behaviors.

The meeting facilitator often looks like the Master of Ceremonies at the meeting. He will frequently be walking around in front of the room, wielding a black marking pen and verbally rewarding members for their contributions. But his job is much more complicated than that of an emcee. He is constantly monitoring the quality and quantity of each member's contribution and, at the same time, evaluating the current quality of the product being developed.

He needs to know how to keep members on target and also needs the ability to see when a seemingly off-target remark might be worth pursuing. Most of the communication in a facilitated meeting is in a "Hub and Spoke" pattern. The meeting facilitator is the Hub and information is transmitted to him. He sends the information to the other team members, who are at the end of their "spokes." He requests opinions from others until a decision is made and then he records it. While it is possible to interact with each other, the members typically find it easier to respond to the meeting facilitator like a teacher conducting a class discussion, sending and receiving information along their private spoke.

The primary goal of the meeting facilitator is to get the group to accomplish their task effectively. While the facilitator demonstrates how to run a meeting, members may pick up some tips on how to more effectively run their own meetings. However, this learning is incidental and not one of the main goals of the meeting facilitator. The meeting facilitator is not tasked with improving the future functioning of the work group.

b. Team Facilitation

The "team facilitator" takes a more active role in the life of the team than does the meeting facilitator, and team facilitator requires an additional set of skills beyond those of a meeting facilitator. The context in which the team facilitator works is the decision-making group. The team facilitator also helps the team focus on the task at hand.

However, it is the team facilitator's primary mission that is different. That mission is to develop the team's abilities rather than merely to help them accomplish the task at hand.

The team facilitator has a set of over-riding goals:

- Making the team a better functioning unit by improving their team atmosphere
- Improving their procedures
- Encouraging collaboration
- Dealing with membership issues
- Improving their communications
- Developing their skills at facilitating their own meetings

The development of the team is more important than the task that they happen to be working on at the time. The most observable difference in behavior revolves around task focus. While the meeting facilitator's primary task is to sharpen focus on the task, the team facilitator may draw the team away from its task in service of improving the team's long-term functioning.

The team facilitator may call for a stop in the action to highlight something that has happened. This type of intervention is attempted when the facilitator believes that focusing on the process illustrated by the recent action will result in the team's learning more than they would accomplish than if they moved forward on the task itself. These judgments are made on-the-fly, require considerable training, experience, and a strong basis in Intervention Theory (see Secret 10 below).

Intervention Theory is the theoretical basis upon which the team facilitator makes his choice of intervention in the life of the group. There are many interventions possible at any given point. The team facilitator has to have a mental picture of what things the group needs to learn in order to improve their effectiveness, and he must make a professional judgment about whether a current situation which has popped up in the normal course of their team life presents an opportunity for the team to learn. Then the facilitator must decide whether or not to intervene.

The intervention can take many forms, depending on the team facilitator's estimate of the team members' maturity and ability to accept the learning. The decision of how to intervene is governed by the team facilitator's professional judgment of which outcome the team is capable of achieving.

As the team-building progresses, the members of the team gradually learn to make their own interventions in order to improve the working of the team. The team intervening on its own and the team facilitator making fewer and fewer interventions is a process that occurs simultaneously. When the team no longer needs professional team facilitation, then it is ready to continue on its own, and the team-building intervention is completed.

Use of the Two Definitions of Facilitation by the Team Leader

Leadership INSIGHT requires both definitions of facilitation to be used extensively by the team leader. The leader of a team will always need to keep an eye on how efficiently the team meeting is running. In addition, because the team leader has a picture of how the team and its members should function, he/she can differentiate between a momentary loss of focus and a more serious problem that the team may be facing.

As the leader of the work team, you must have a clear idea of what learning they need to achieve to become a championship team. Developing a clear list of items to be achieved will also allow you to decide how to best guide your team.

If the team development has been going on for a considerable amount of time and significant progress has been made, you might decide that *this particular situation requires* the use of meeting facilitation to move the team toward the accomplishment of their immediate task.

On the other hand, you might evaluate the same situation as a chance to get some long-term growth for the team, and decide that such an accomplishment is more valuable than the immediate task. In that case, you might decide to view the situation as one requiring team facilitation, which could slow the team in achieving the immediate task, but might move them considerably in terms of their growth as a developing championship team.

Such decisions are difficult to make and are even more difficult because they must be made on-the-fly. It is important to understand that, as your team develops, it will become more robust. This robustness means that if you make a mistake in the above-described choice, it will not doom the team to mediocrity. It may cost you an opportunity, but it will virtually never cost you the team's future. Team behavior tends to be repetitive. It will happen again. Other opportunities will arise. Do not worry about an opportunity missed!

Phillip E. Rosner, Ph.D.

Secret 9. Critical Incidents (CI)

Teams do not have to be taught how to function. Put several people in a room, give them a task, tell them what the output should look like, give them a time limit, and they will not sit there in silence for the next three hours. Sustained silence (which is a critical incident, in itself) causes discomfort in many groups – especially in its early stages. It is not tolerated well. Within a few seconds in the life of a new team, someone will make an attempt to provide direction. Any kind of distracting task will alleviate the tension caused by silence.

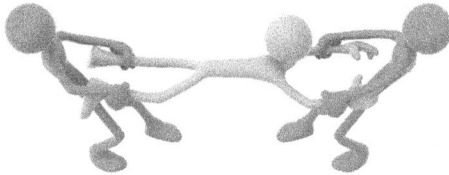

It does not matter if the direction is useful or not. What matters is that it removes the discomfort of silence and doing nothing. The most frequent way this is done is by someone suggesting that "we tell who we are and what specialties we have." This gives everyone a chance to talk in a very structured way and might provide some useful information. It matters little that almost every time you have done that exercise in the past, you have found that the information is seldom worth remembering and have obtained a minimal amount of information about each person. The "introducing ourselves" tactic is an task that is easy to accept and better than silence.

The awkward silence itself was a simple critical incident. It was "critical" in that it affected the group and required something to be done to alleviate the tension. It was an "incident" in that most people in the group knew that it had happened.

The history and usage of critical incidents has been well documented in Cohen & Smith (1976). They define a Critical Incident (CI) as a situation that is perceived as affecting the group and leads to a choice point in the life of the group. The question of whether to intervene and how to do so is suddenly thrust upon the group members or the group leader. Some CIs are obvious while others are very subtle.

The most obvious CI is heralded by a sudden and complete silence during a work session.

It may only last a second or two, but it happens, and everyone is aware of its occurrence.

In the first meeting of a new work team, the nominal team leader starts with a general statement of work and says, "Let's start working on this topic by throwing out ideas and writing them on the board." One of the members immediately responds with, "That's a terrible idea. I don't know even half the people in this room. Let's find out who we are first, before we do meaningless brainstorming."

An instantaneous and awkward silence hit the group, and remained for what seemed to be an eternity (actual time: about 5 seconds). Everyone heard the words, "terrible idea" and "meaningless brainstorming," and knew it to be an insult to the leader's authority. The tension in the room was palpable.

The incident was not caused by the act of rejecting the leader's suggestion itself. It was caused by the emotionally loaded manner and choice of words used in the rejection. If the member had said, "That sounds like a great way to start, but I would feel better if we could introduce ourselves first," there might not have been an incident at all.

The CI lasts so long because team members are thinking about the issues of confrontation (with the leader), wondering what behaviors will be tolerated in the group, considering the atmosphere of the team (aggressive and confrontational or accepting and friendly) and asking themselves if such a confrontation will at some later time be directed toward them.

Other Critical Incidents are not so easy to see. They can happen quickly and can be covered over rapidly. This makes an appropriate intervention more difficult.

> *The work team is trying to list the elements of a project in order of the need for completion (in order to perform the next step). The first three items were proposed, shortly discussed, and quickly adopted with a loose consensus. Susan quietly calls out her idea for #4 followed by a second of silence, after which Richard loudly calls out his idea. The group responds to Richard's idea, starts discussing it, and doesn't even acknowledge that Susan said anything.*

This example too is a Critical Incident for several reasons. Susan's idea was rejected without being acknowledged. It told her that she didn't count as far as the group was concerned. Other less outgoing members of the group may have gotten a message about whether everyone has an equal right to be heard (a membership issue). Some of the more outgoing members may have learned a lesson that says, "Volume overcomes ideas" (a team norm). Lots of messages can be interpreted from this CI, but the key notion is that the group is at a choice point: Does someone say something or not? If yes, who says it and what should be said?

The way one decides whether to say something and what to say is discussed in detail in the next section: Intervention Theory. Whether something is done about a critical incident will have a profound effect on the life and the character of the team. The leader or the team members can influence the culture of the team profoundly by the quality and kind of interventions that occur. What is important is *to be aware of the Critical Incidents*, in general, and *to recognize the quality and impact of them* specifically.

In developing Leadership INSIGHT, one must listen and observe carefully. The bottom line is that these incidents do occur. They are signs that something is happening in the group.

Developing Leadership INSIGHT in order to see these Critical Incidents is the first step in correcting the direction of the group.

Use of Critical Incidents (CIs) by the Team Leader

Critical Incidents are most frequently used in two ways:

- As a signal that something is happening, and
- As a framework for learning when and how to intervene.

As A Signal

Critical Incidents occur because emotions are involved. If a group member suggests that the leader, who has previously acknowledged that he is unfamiliar with the topic being discussed, should appoint a topic specialist to lead the discussion, there will be no collective group gasp. It will not be seen as a challenge to the leader's authority. It will be seen as an appropriate contribution and a viable option.

On the other hand, if the leader thinks that he *is* a topic expert, such a suggestion may be received much differently, by both the team and its leader. It would be seen as a CI if the team sees it as a challenge to the leader, his authority or his handling of the team task. Additionally, the tension in the group may increase unless it is dealt with.

As a signal that something is happening, the leader can chose several ways of dealing with it. The least growth-producing way is to ignore it. This is not the same as choosing to delay dealing with it – a conscious, thought-through decision to not intervene right away. Exactly how to choose an intervention will be discussed in the next concept, Intervention Theory.

As a Learning Framework

Typically, the signal is received by several members of the team at the same time. The leader's task is to quickly determine what the Critical Incident means and make a tentative decision as to whether to acknowledge it and how to deal with it. Depending on the stage of development of the group, the context of the CI, and several other factors, the leader decides on a possible intervention.

The general rule of thumb is that the leader should at least acknowledge the CI publically, if it seems that everyone else has seen it occur. To not acknowledge the CI is equivalent of telling the group, "Things will happen in our group that everyone will see, but we will occasionally pretend that they never occurred." Since, in reality, everyone knows that it happened, it makes little sense to pretend it did not. Reality-avoidance is rarely an appropriate strategy.

Acknowledgment of the CI is often a great place to start an intervention to help the team improve their process. The exact direction in which to proceed will depend on a number of factors which we will discuss in the next section.

Phillip E. Rosner, Ph.D.

Secret 10. Intervention Theory

Anytime the leader or another member says or does something that is intended to have an effect on the team, they are performing an intervention. It is done frequently. People say things to influence the group. They also say things to show their expertise. They say things to agree or disagree with what another person in the group has said. However, the insightful leader always has the long-term benefit of the group in mind when an intervention is attempted.

Leadership INSIGHT includes knowing how to intervene when the team's interaction appears to require it. This is not to imply that every good leader must be an expert team facilitator. Leadership INSIGHT does require a solid basic understanding of the principles of intervention theory and how it is used. The primary benefit of this knowledge is to serve as a guide to the leader who is searching for actions to take within the group to help it find solutions.

There are several systematic theories of when and how to intervene when facilitating a team. While I don't advocate the use of any one system over another, my personal choice is the Intervention Cube (Cohen and Smith, 1976). It allows me to choose among 28 possible interventions and further allows me to make the decision as to which of the 28 choices to use in a matter of seconds. (There is also a 29th choice possible – silence. The choice to NOT intervene is always made intentionally, not because one doesn't know what to do.)

Intervention Theory as a Guide

I have found that the great majority of people who call themselves team facilitators (as defined above), *do not have any systematic intervention theory to which they subscribe.* When I have asked the question of people with that title, more than half *did not recognize the term.*

There are two problems with not having a well-practiced intervention theory:

1. The first problem is that it would seem uncomfortable, as a professional, to be winging it all the time. There is no way to predict what will come up in a group discussion -- therefore, relying on past experience alone, without a guide, seems to introduce a somewhat random element to the process.

2. The second problem involves the long-term need to acquaint the members with facilitation so that eventually they can self-facilitate the group. If you don't have and use an intervention theory, how can you teach the group to facilitate itself when you are no longer available to them?

The guiding part of Leadership INSIGHT is the knowledge of how to intervene in the life of the team in order to help them toward becoming a high-performance and championship team. Understanding and practicing the use of an intervention model is a basic tool for this purpose.

A young woman asked me to supervise her postdoctoral internship in Organizational Development Psychology. She wanted a special emphasis on team development. When asked, she told me that she had not learned any specific intervention theory. When I asked how she chose between the many thousands of possible interventions, her reply was, "I remember what my professor did in the groups he ran in my presence. He was great at doing interventions.

My obvious next question was, "What will you do when a never-before-seen critical incident occurs?" Her response was a blank stare followed by, "I'm sure that something will come to me."

The young woman had seen what her professor did, but she did not know why each intervention was chosen. She did not clearly see that the chosen intervention was not merely a response to what had occurred previously. It had an intention; a desired result. That intervention was an educated response to all of the team's previous history, its current state of group maturity, and the desired outcome that the professor hoped for. Without some intervention theory to rely upon, the young woman would be mimicking what she had seen (or thought that she remembered seeing), not what was intended.

A Basic Intervention Model

Cohen and Smith (1976) present their Intervention Theory model at the level needed to train professional facilitators to intervene in a wide variety of groups. I am presenting a much simplified version of that model at about the level that I use to present the model to an executive team nearing the end of their team-building program. It is presented to them so they can understand the complexity of deciding how to intervene in the life of a group and provide some guidance. It also allows them to develop insight into the interventions they have seen me use in their group.

Note of caution: If the reader would like to become proficient in the use of this model or any other model, what follows is not enough! Go to the original source and learn the theory in much greater detail. If you still would like to learn to actually put these into action, find a mentor, a professional team facilitator, and learn to do it correctly. Intervening in the life of a work team always has consequences – to do so as a professional requires training.

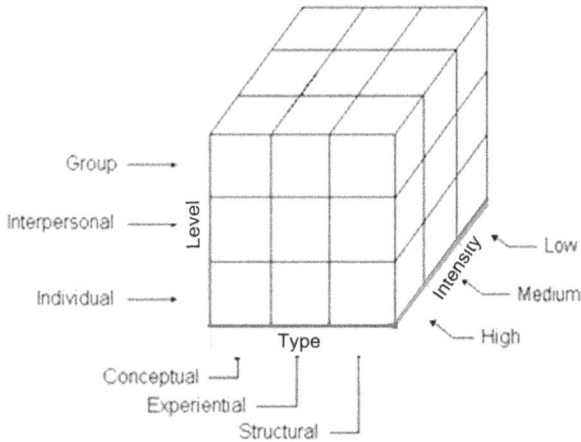

The Cohen-Smith Intervention Cube

Level

As discussed in Secret 3 – Multiple Levels of Behavior, there are things happening in the group to multiple combinations of members simultaneously. The first decision to be made is to what part of the team will I direct this intervention? The choice of which level to direct the intervention is usually (but not always) obvious. The three levels in a basic model are:

1. An intervention to the group as a whole.

This level is chosen when the intervention's target is the entire group. It is directed to them as a team. (e.g. – "It seems to me that the team, without actually saying the words, is trying to …"

2. To 2 or more people at the same time (Interpersonal).

If 2 or 3 people are involved, that subgroup is probably the right place at which to aim. This level is chosen when the intervention is used to help the subgroup. (e.g. – "Are you, Sam and Barbara attempting to…?"

3.   To an Individual.

If the Critical Incident (CI) involves only one person, the individual level is probably correct. This level is chosen when the individual is the target of the intervention. (e.g. – "Charlie, you seem to be having trouble with…".

Whatever level is chosen will have consequences. As the intervention choice moves from Group toward Individual level, the intensity of its effect on the individual increases. An individual level intervention allows the other team members to watch the action. This will allow the non-involved people to learn by watching the person to whom the intervention is directed.

There is no rule that says the intervention level must match the level of the critical incident. The facilitator may choose to intervene at a different level depending on the particular goal that he/she is trying to accomplish.

> *On the first day of a team-building effort (projected to take 9 to 12 months to complete), an individual member (we'll call her Ann) broke a short silence saying: "I am thrilled that we are doing this, because I have a lot of personal problems in my life. I believe that this will allow me to talk about them in detail and that this will be more effective than my therapy sessions."*
>
> *The instantaneous intake of breath was spectacular and the silence that followed was palpable. Clearly a critical incident had occurred, but what intervention should I choose?*

At that moment the life of the group had been measured in minutes. No one on the team was certain about what we were actually supposed to do. The ability of the group to effectively deal with emotional issues was unknown, but should be assumed to be minimal. The group had frozen at the thought of spending these days as an intense therapy session. Additionally, Ann had spoken a sincere message of appreciation for the help she thought would come and her real need for that help.

The decision as to choice of level was relatively easy. Although the CI came from an individual, there were few choices of individual interventions that would deal with the problem and leave the group unscathed. Talking to her about her expectations of using the group as a therapy provider and delving into her problems was out of the question.

The choice was to deal with the CI at the group level. Choosing that level took the pressure off of the speaker (who was obviously aware of the effect of her words) and focused on what these kinds of groups typically do. This provided the group with needed information and redirected the spotlight from the speaker. Because this was a work team, therapy-type issues are rarely discussed. By directing the intervention toward the group, I got this message to Ann without having to focus on and possibly embarrass her.

Type

The next decision is what form will the intervention take? This has to do with the actual form of the intervention. The Cohen and Smith model uses three types of interventions with an almost infinite variation of content within each type. The content is less important than the structure of the intervention. They are conceptual, experiential, and structural interventions.

1. Conceptual Interventions

A conceptual intervention is one that is directed at the intellect. Its immediate target is the understanding of a concept. When used purely for this purpose, it sounds like an explanation of something or a discourse on a topic. It can also be used to lower the intensity of a CI. For example, in the above example of Ann wanting her own therapy group, the facilitator could say to the group "We all come to this group with various ideas and desires. Since we don't know exactly what the rules are, anything is possible. What we talk about will usually be decided by the group as a whole and changes in direction are usually done by consent. What do you all think we should be doing?"

In general, conceptual interventions engage the receivers' thinking and tend to disengage emotions. This type of intervention can be used to redirect the focus of the discussion or change the level.

2. Experiential Interventions

Experiential interventions get their name from the expected outcome desired – the group members experience something as people. They can be directed at any level and are designed to focus on having a personal experience rather than developing an intellectual understanding.

> *"Imagine what it would be like to be in a meeting and discover that you are unable to communicate your thoughts and ideas to the others in the group. Focus on what you are hearing and what you feel when you try to say something or write something and no one understands you."*)

The intervention strives for as detailed an image as possible and typically ends with a discussion of what people felt rather than what they thought. This kind of imaging shows them that their heads can be both thought-oriented and emotion-oriented.

3. Structural Interventions

Structural interventions often include physically changing the structure of the group or subgroup. (e.g. – the group could break into subgroups of three each and sit in separate areas of the room.) In addition to the re-forming, a task could be given focusing on the specific learnings to be achieved. A time limit is usually set and a discussion of what happened during the intervention by the other group members is typical.

Structural interventions are frequently used to illustrate important content in a physical way. For example, trust can frequently be an issue in work teams. A structural intervention that asks the members to close their eyes and freely fall backward and be caught by other members (a Trust Fall) can be very potent in illustrating that the other members of the team can be trusted. It can also result in a member learning that they are or are not capable of giving trust easily.

One of my clients decided to do a structural, group-level intervention as a team-building exercise. The president of the company assigned each of his senior executive team members to one of four groups. Each group received a budget and the task of building a deer hunting blind on a property they had leased for several hunting seasons.

The results were four hunting blinds that were well-constructed in four totally different ways, and also enough discussion about the exercise to last for days. It was a solid structural intervention.

Intensity

The final decision point is the intensity of the intervention. This refers to the expected degree of the impact of the intervention. It is a decision that is really a professional judgment of what degree of intensity will move the group in a growth direction fastest with a minimal risk of hurting the group. Too intense an intervention and the group could experience a setback. Too little intensity and the group might not progress as fast as it could have.

The intensity of an intervention is typically addressed by either the instructions accompanying an intervention or the manner in which the intervention is made.

An example of the use of instructions would be a structural intervention regarding "openness and sharing." The group breaks into pairs and interviews each other. Several examples of different instructions and the intensity levels that might follow.

1. Low Intensity

"Ask your partner to tell you three things about yourself that no one in the group knows. Afterwards your partner will tell the group those things about you." The Low Intensity intervention is the kind of "icebreaker" that is frequently used in meetings. The information revealed is shallow and typical of what might be revealed on an insurance form - name, rank, serial number. It gets the people talking to each other, establishes that we share information with the group and establishes that in this group, we can talk about things that go beyond the usual. All this is done with a minimal perceived threat to the self.

2. Medium Intensity

"Interview your partner in order to prepare a group introduction. Do NOT include anything having to do with geography, relationships with others including family, history or numbers. Afterwards the partners will introduce each other to the group." The Medium Intensity instructions eliminate most of the easy things to tell about yourself – where you lived, number of family members, your biography, or how long you have done something. It forces you to think about whom you are and to tell the interviewer about what you are really like. You are still unlikely to reveal any deep, dark secrets, but you will have to reveal more than you normally would about yourself. Thoughts about possible perceived threats are not uncommon.

3. High Intensity

"Your doctor has just informed you that you are about to die. You are being interviewed in order to prepare the eulogy for your funeral. Those people who know you are gone. The only memories of you on earth will be what you tell this person. After the exercise, your eulogy will be read to the group."

The High Intensity instructions are by their nature, somewhat dark. They are designed to cause you to think about things you we seldom address – and you are supposed to tell them to a relative stranger – who will then relay them to the group. The decision about what to reveal may be fraught with tension.

Interviewee Behavior

The behavior of the interviewee during data collection is the subject of all three intensities. What you choose to tell about yourself (and what you choose to hide) reveals your level of openness. The other objective of such an exercise is to establish that in this group, we share more than we usually do.

These types of interventions are not significantly different from the interventions that a team manager does during the course of a day. They are done in the same way – in order to effect a behavior change (or behavior continuance). As with the other kinds of interventions, the level of intensity is chosen to have a desired effect. Responsible judgment in this selection is critical. The group must be ready for the intensity you select.

A Message to the Team Leader Regarding the Intervention Cube

The Cohen-Smith Intervention Cube is one of several intervention theories and models. The intervention strategy that a team leader uses is a personal choice that they must make. I have seen intervention theories with which I did not agree, but have not seen one that would not work adequately if applied systematically.

The above presentation of the Intervention Cube is done to give the team leader a taste of the complexity of intervening in the life of a team. It is important to understand that all interventions have consequences. If the team leader thinks about what intervention to use and its desired consequences before it is employed, that leader is more likely to select an effective intervention.

The important idea is that as you interact with your team, you think about what you are going to do and about what outcome you want to achieve. You will not always hit the mark with every intervention, but you will improve over time.

Leadership INSIGHT arms you with the knowledge of how groups work and how your actions cause them to respond. As you develop your Leadership INSIGHT, your decisions will become more effective and you will move your team more in the direction of high performance.

Secret 11. Modeling Behavior

Being the Team Leader/Boss

The team leader has a unique and somewhat awkward role. Actually, he/she has multiple roles, some of which are intentional and some are forced by the team. Because the team has a member in the room who is their boss, it is natural that they would look to that person for direction. As the leader, you may have more experience or knowledge; it is easy to slip into the role of direction-giver. If all you desired was a group of automatons who followed your directions and carried out orders blindly, the direction-giver role would be fine. But you must resist that easy path if you want to develop a championship team.

I have never heard the words, "I'm the boss and you will do it my way." However, the behavior of the group when the leader says something clearly indicates that they are aware of the status of the boss. If the leader makes a comment during the discussion, it will almost always cause an instantaneous change in the course of the discussion.

Trained team leaders understand that their stated opinion typically has a greater impact on the discussion than anyone else's opinion. A common rule taught to team leaders is, "Hold your opinion on the issue until everyone else has spoken." I have found that it is the rare team leader who can wait that long to give an opinion. This is especially true if that leader thinks the discussion is going in a direction he doesn't like. One of the significant decisions a leader must make is whether to provide or hold an opinion or direction.

Research has shown that a team which develops its own decisions tends to be better at carrying out those decisions. If the team is heading toward a decision that you, as leader, think is best – say nothing. It has the same effect as ordering that particular decision with the added benefits of not having to use your positional power to make it happen. Teams that make their own decisions are more likely to execute those decisions well.

Do what I do, NOT what I say

Teams seem to display a kind of natural tendency to follow the leader. In much the same way that children play that game, we have learned that if you do what the leader does, you will be treated favorably. As adults we talk about "Imitation being the most sincere form of flattery." George Bernard Shaw modified that thought saying, "Imitation is not just the sincerest form of flattery – it's the sincerest form of learning."

As team leader, remember that the team will not follow you blindly. They will tend to imitate behavior that is *effective*. If you are respected as the team leader, that may increase the significance of your observed behavior in the eyes of the other team members. Your goal is to increase the team's effectiveness. The most enduring behavior-changing technique is behavior modeling.

During my career as an organizational psychologist, I have sat in on hundreds of team meetings. There have been, of course, considerable variation in how each team leader behaves.

All team members can and will play multiple roles during any given team meeting. The team leader has several options as to how to behave. All of them require skills in modeling behavior. Some examples include the good team member, the non-participant/participant observer, the teacher, and the authority figure.

The good team member

The team member is the most important and easiest role for the team leader and the most difficult role for the rest of the team. In this role, the team leader appears to give up the role of the leader, consistently act as part of the group, and work diligently to model appropriate member behavior. It's often hard for the rest of the team to accept, at least initially, because they would feel more comfortable with him behaving in the way they expect, in a leadership role. It's easier to understand the leader as someone who tells them what to do. Many groups find it extremely difficult to allow their leader to become one of the team members. The team leader must, through observable behavior, establish the team value that allows each member to have more than one role in the group at different times.

The Non-participant/participant observer

Team members, especially in the early stages of team formation, have no problem with group members who choose not to speak much. They have much more trouble dealing with a silent team leader. The knowledgeable team leader must model both roles. The leader must find a way to be the leader while never abandoning the role of observer. The leader has the same rights as the members – among them, the right to speak (or not speak) at their discretion.

It is important to note that a non-participant observer involves two sets of behaviors. The first, non-participation, is relatively easy to do – stop talking and avoid sending positive or negative non-verbal signals in reaction to the discussion. The second role, group observer, is much more difficult. It is not a passive role. One doesn't just sit quietly with eyes open. It involves actively looking at both content and process during the meeting and analyzing its meaning. It is as if you were both sitting in your chair and sitting outside the group looking at it from a short distance.

The Teacher

There will be times when the group needs to learn things didactically. Standing up at a newsprint pad or whiteboard is sometimes the best way to convey complex concepts. Unlike an actual teacher in a classroom, the team leader doesn't act this way on a daily basis. The group isn't expecting such behavior as part of their normal routine. The key question that the team leader must ask is, "Are some of the team members indicating, either through non-participation or through less than appropriate comments, that they are not up-to-speed on the topic?" If so, it is almost always appropriate to suggest a short interruption of the discussion to review the topic and make sure that all team members have all the appropriate information.

Most trained team leaders use the mini-lecture format, which typically takes 2-5 minutes to illustrate a point or to illuminate a situation. The choice of who delivers the material should always be in favor of the team member who has the most specific expert knowledge. While in theory, any member of the group could do the exact same thing, this method is rarely used by a non-leader. Here is an example of its use by both:

In the latter stages of a senior executive team-building program, the team leader (CEO) intervened in a discussion and said to his Senior Vice-presidents, "It seems to me that we may not all be equally aware of the details of the background for this discussion. Is that right?" When the group acknowledged that that was the case, he then asked "Carrie, you are the most knowledgeable on this topic, could you stand up and give us a 2 or 3 minutes review of that background, so we all have the same information?"

After Carrie delivered her impromptu presentation, there were several people who made comments that they were glad this had happened, because they were hesitant to show their lack of knowledge of the topic.

Authority/Authority figure

There is a difference between an authority and an authority figure. An authority is typically seen as someone with special knowledge. The term "authority figure" implies someone with potential power over a group that is independent of that person's knowledge. At times, the two are related in that having special knowledge might imbue the possessor with greater potential power. The team leader must walk the tightrope between having a lot of information and exercising power.

> *The CEO of a client organization with which I was working felt somewhat pressed for time with regard to a complex decision that her senior team had to make. Just before the meeting she said to me, "I'm not certain why we are having this meeting today. I know what decision we need to make. Wouldn't it be more efficient for me to just announce the program and assign tasks to my team members?"*

> *I told her that there were two problems with her statement and question. "First, it assumes that your solution is the best possible one. That may or may not be true. There may be a better solution that you haven't thought of, or your team may be able to refine your plan and make it even better."*

> *"Second, even if your solution is, in reality, the best solution, it will require the entire team to be committed to its implementation. Research and real-world experience has shown that participation and consensus on a given plan results in much more commitment to the final result than only presenting a plan and expecting commitment."*

Modeling behavior by the team leader is a very strong method by which to send messages. It is more subtle than announcing that "we should do more of this kind of behavior or less of that kind." The other team members can watch the behavior and assess its effects. It also reinforces the idea that the Boss can behave in different ways. This encourages them to behave in different ways and assess how well it works for them.

Use of Modeling Behavior by the Insightful Leader.

The first step in developing your behavior modeling skills is to assess your current status. How do you typically behave in this team? Start answering the question by trying to visualize your last few meetings. Try to see your behavior from the team members' points of view. What did you do and what did you say? How did the team react to you?

Next, take written notes of how you behave in the next few team meetings and how the team members reacted to that behavior. (Understand that no matter how hard you try, your behavior will change to some degree merely because you are doing this exercise.) After the meeting evaluate yourself. What did you do that worked well? What didn't work as planned?

Before your next meeting, think about one or two behaviors you would like to model. Try to visualize how that would look and try it out. Evaluate yourself after the meeting and repeat.

When you are thinking about what to model in the next session, start to look at what behavior changes you would like to see on the parts of the other members. Try modeling those.

This process is slow, but such learning tends to last. They become part of the members' repertoire of behavior. Changing a team into a championship team is a long-term process.

Secret 12: Decision-Making: Cooperation vs. Collaboration

Cooperation is the achievement of a task by dividing it among participants, who work together as individuals in support of each other's goals. A new result can be created, but it is the collective work of individuals not a team effort.

Collaboration is the achievement of a task by the interaction of participants, who align their goals, coordinate their efforts and develop a shared vision of the outcome. They work to achieve shared ownership of the result through the accommodation of the perspectives of all members through discussion and negotiation.

The core difference between cooperation and collaboration revolves around the need for a collaborative group to understand the differences in approach and philosophy between the various members of the group and resolve them. In essence, the collaborative group is *developing a common set of assumptions and working philosophies that all members can comfortably share.* This must be done for a team to establish a long-term collaborative atmosphere. To do this, all members of the team must have considerable respect for one another and develop a sense of we-ness as they find common ground to share.

This is an option and not a requirement for co-operating groups. They have each been given a part of the puzzle to solve, and have each committed to do their work as professionally as possible. The other members of the team trust that this will be done. There is, however, no pressing need to adopt a common set of values and a common philosophy. Each person can perform at a solid effectiveness level in their own silo, as long as the individual pieces of the problem are well-defined and they have functions that are independent of each other.

Cooperation works relatively well until different pieces of the total solution do not fit together. It is at this point that conflict may arise due to different approaches to implementing the decision. At that point, there will be a need to go back to underlying assumptions and approaches and develop a more collaborative model.

Important differences in types of decision-making

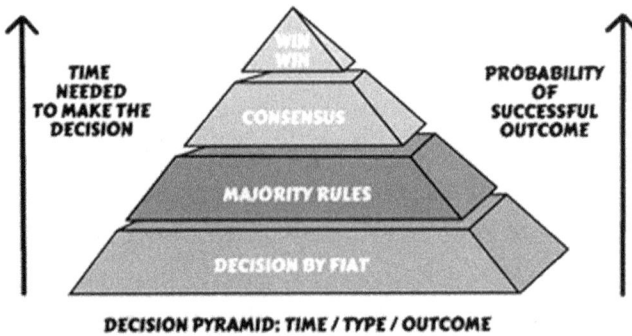

DECISION PYRAMID: TIME / TYPE / OUTCOME

Decision by fiat

A decision is made by your superiors and handed down to your team. Your team task is to make it happen. There is no participation in the decision by the people who will be tasked with carrying out the decision.

Think about "The Charge of the Light Brigade" by Alfred, Lord Tennyson.

"Theirs not to reason why,
Theirs but to do and die."

While life and death decisions and need for instant execution of tasks are rare in today's corporate world, some team leaders will still ask their team to carry out a task without question or comment. It has been my experience that blind obedience by corporate executives and their teams is seldom comfortable.

When time is critical (as is often the case in the military during combat) decision by fiat may be necessary. The decision-making superior is assumed to have evaluated all relevant information and made the best decision possible.

The team members are trained to avoid evaluation of the appropriateness of the orders. They are trained to respond as ordered. Cooperation is required, collaboration is not.

Decision by vote – Also known as "majority rules."

When the team is asked to vote on possible alternative methods, a simple majority is most frequently employed. Most people are familiar with the process. A discussion is held, followed by a vote. The one of several alternatives with the most votes is the one that prevails.

This procedure has some clear advantages:

Team members feel that they have had a chance to speak. This is not a small thing. Satisfaction with the decision increases as the level of participation increases. Resentment toward the decision increases when people feel that they have not been allowed to have their say.

It is relatively rapid process. Since a vote can be taken at any time, the discussion can be long or short. The final decision is made by a simple count of the votes.

There are also disadvantages. For example, there is an expectation that the team members on the losing side will immediately support the decision made, even though they were arguing against it just moments before. This expectation is more or less warranted depending on the importance of the decision to them.

Some of the members on the "losing side" may feel that the discussion was cut off prematurely. In other words, they may think, "If the discussion was allowed to continue, my point of view would have eventually been accepted."

The most serious flaw is that members whose position did not prevail will be tasked with executing a decision that they believe is wrong. It is naïve to believe that people will work whole-heartedly on a decision that they think won't work.

Experience has shown that open examination of a failed project often reveals that the sources of failure can be attributed to team members who argued against the project. These people typically have not caused the failure consciously. It doesn't take much effort to cause a team to fail. I've seen a team fail when only one or two members give the project a 90% effort.

In a team discussion about a major software development project which was very behind schedule, various departments were complaining about each other having failed to meet the schedule to finish their part of the project. (If a group needs your completed work to start theirs, your lateness often make them late also.)

Several unhappy project managers mentioned that two of the worst offenders had voted against the project originally. Later in the discussion, it was discovered that the two managers in question were not only late in the delivery of their pieces of the project, but also they had not alerted the receiving managers that their work would be delayed. This caused the receiving managers to be unable to schedule other work for their people to do while waiting for the missing pieces.

No one on the team believed that the two offenders were late with their pieces of the project intentionally. But their original vote against the project and the lack of notification of lateness did not go unnoticed.

"Majority rules" can be used when the decision is not critical. No one would consciously or subconsciously sabotage a decision involving what kind of pizza to order for lunch or what color to paint an office. The decision does not have enough gravity for the members to care tremendously one way or the other.

The procedure "majority rules" is not the best procedure to use when the project depends on the full, committed effort of each team member in order to succeed, because it does not do anything about the effects of losing on the minority.

Decision by Consensus

Consensus is a process in which group members develop and agree to support a decision in the best interest of the whole. Consensus is a method of making a decision as well as a kind of decision. Seeking consensus is the effort to decide on a course of action that can be agreed upon by all parties who will be affected by the decision.

The primary advantage of consensus-seeking by teams is that each member is considered in the decision. A collaborative solution is sought in which each team member votes "yes" only when they feel that they can support the final decision at least to some extent. This criterion forces the team, as a whole, to focus on the objections of dissenting member. There is no question on the part of that dissenting member that his/her objections were ignored. Compromises are considered until all can vote "yes".

Consensus is not the same as unanimity. Consensus-seeking involves working to find a solution to a problem that approaches meeting all the needs of all parties involved. Only very unique solutions, covering all members' needs totally, will be adopted unanimously.

The Best of all Decision Worlds: The Win/win Decision

A win-win decision is one in which each party gains from the decision. It involves searching for a unique decision that actually satisfies all parties. A win-win decision is different from compromise. Compromise implies losing to some degree -- giving up something in order to reach a decision. A compromise solution runs the risk of fully pleasing no one as a solution to a problem.

Consensus is a process of exploration to find the best solution that meets the needs of the group. Unless everyone who is necessary to the successful implementation of the decision is able to commit to it, it can be sabotaged. Members who are not really committed to the decision may not put forth a maximum effort. These less-than-committed members could consciously or subconsciously cause a decision to fail.

When all team members can whole-heartedly support a decision, it is more likely to be executed well and its goals accomplished. Taking the time to find a solution to a problem that everyone can be enthusiastic about might take extra time, but it is more likely to succeed.

How to Reach a Win-Win Decision

The first step in the process is to recognize when the decision-making process is blocked. The most common symptom occurs when two or more apparently incompatible decisions remain the last alternatives and sides are being taken by the group members. This is a classic intra-group conflict. It is often realized when the group discussion is seen to be repeating itself. People on both sides are repeating the same arguments without any effect.

To break the repetitive behavior, the team changes the focus of the discussion. Instead of arguing the merits and disadvantages of each solution for the nth time, the leader redirects the group to talk about what each side is trying to achieve by each solution. In essence, the two sides are focusing on what a solution should do for the team. Both sides can look at their two solutions in terms how well the ultimate aims are achieved.

When the aims of the ideal solution are clear, an exploration of a new possible solution commences in order to find one that meets all (or most) of these aims. Whatever negative feelings that might have been generated during the previous discussion are wiped clean because now you are seeking something else. Everyone is clear that the object is to find a solution that best fits the aims.

When a win-win solution is found, it has the positive characteristics of meeting all of the aims of the group optimally. No one wins while the other loses the battle. The decision is made when all of the underlying concerns of the members have been met. Everybody wins.

Use of decision-making by the team leader with Leadership INSIGHT

In the planning of any project or task, there are numerous decisions that a team must make. Just because this is an important piece of the actual work, this does not mean that the leader must avoid using this as a team learning opportunity. The leader has several general rules to follow in order to improve the effectiveness of those decisions.

For example, estimate the time available for the team to make the decision and carry it out. If the time is available, help the team move toward a more effective solution.

Decide if you want the team to have a longer-range learning experience. If that is your goal, allow yourself to model appropriate member behavior and guide the team toward a win-win goal. Caution: Don't rush it! Let the team move there with the minimum push on your part.

Try to play devil's advocate. If they don't see that their decision is less than optimal, point it out to them.

Softly make it clear to them that you are (and they should be) looking for a decision that gets the job done and that everyone can agree to support.

The team leader should (informally) move the group in the direction of a unanimous win/win decision. At least, help the team avoid any solution that places one or more members in a position in which they will have to carry out critical tasks that they (apparently) don't agree should be undertaken.

When a solid decision is reached, reward the team vigorously. It's hard work seeking win-win decisions. When a team reaches (or closely approximates one) tell them that you understand what they've done and that you appreciate their effort and the quality of their decision.

Chapter Summary

The purpose of this chapter is to discuss how a leader develops the team while achieving the appropriate task result. Leadership INSIGHT focuses on developing the skills that get results both in the long-term and the short-term. Essentially, the focus is on how to use these task situations to improve the way a team functions on the next task.

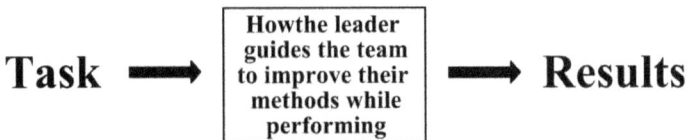

Task ➡ **How the leader guides the team to improve their methods while performing** ➡ **Results**

Two sets of concepts are discussed: The first set (Team Facilitation, Critical Incidents and Intervention Theory) are rarely discussed outside of training environments designed for developing professional group facilitators. Yet I believe that they are critical concepts for team leaders to understand in order to select how to intervene in the life of their team. They provide background which can be used to go beyond simply helping the team with their assigned tasks. They empower the team leader to recognize when the team has a problem, know when a corrective action is needed, and decide what intervention to use.

Team facilitation provides a map for what a championship team looks like and how it behaves. As the team leader continually assesses the development of the team, the leader can plan which areas of need should be worked upon.

Critical Incidents show both the leader and the team members when something important has just happened. These happenings in the life of a team are often ignored. This concept needs to be understood in order for the team leader to recognize them for what they are and, more importantly, to see them as a cue that tells the leader that (perhaps) something should be done to address the incident. They tell the leader when it might be possible to move the team more towards championship status.

Intervention theory is discussed and a single model is presented in some detail. The message to be learned is: When the team leader intervenes in the life of the team, the intended outcome should be selected before making the intervention, and the leader should understand the wide variety of possible interventions that can be chosen.

The final two concepts (Modeling Behavior and Decision-making) are more general, while retaining importance as skills for the leader. Modeling behavior is a constant task for the leader. It needs to become second nature to him/her. Decision-making is the heart of most of the work of the team. Almost all discussions are designed to achieve some result and the manner of achieving the final decision is critical. When the decisions are made optimally, the probability of their achievement rises dramatically.

Phillip E. Rosner, Ph.D.

Chapter SEVEN
Now you SEE it – Before you didn't!

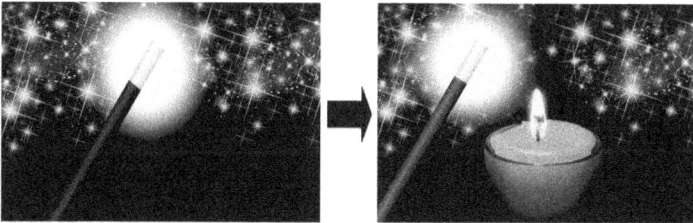

This chapter title is obviously a play on words from the magician's patter, "Now you see it, now you don't!" as something magically disappears. I chose to use these words because to a small extent, gaining Leadership INSIGHT is like that -- a little like magic. You didn't see it before – now you do!

After a while, you will have difficulty remembering what you used to *not see*. The amount of energy required to use these tools will drop dramatically, and their use will become automatic. Leadership INSIGHT will become a part of you.

You have learned to see below the surface of your team. You can appreciate that your team is multi-dimensional. You can better see how they operate as individuals, subgroups and as a functioning team. You can better see the effects of things that happen during team work sessions on the individuals and the team. Finally, you have learned more about how to change your team's behavior.

Much of my training in psychology graduate school was along the lines of what I have shown to you, my readers. The applied psychologist is expected to:

- Diagnose the situation
- Discover the underlying problem (*not* the presenting problem)
- Understand what needs to be changed
- Know how to bring about the change
- Help the client actually make the change.

The psychologist is expected to see below the surface and be prepared to make appropriate corrective changes. In doing so, the psychologist must allow the person or organization to make those changes in a more or less permanent way.

The role of a team leader is much the same.

The team leader is expected to:

- See what is happening in the team and recognize when the team is not functioning optimally
- Be able to see clearly what is happening below the surface in order to discover the actual underlying problems
- Know how effective teams operate and be prepared to understand the changes that need to be made
- Understand the natural tendencies of teams in order to help direct the team toward more effective performance,
- Have intervention skills which will help move the team toward adopting those changes

You have now been introduced to all of these secrets. You have begun a trip along a road that leads to better understanding of people as they interact with each other. Most of your world consists of people interacting with each other, so you now have a distinct advantage over those who are unaware of these concepts. Use them to better yourself and those around you.

You have been changed permanently by the simple act of knowing about these secrets. You will never again be able to hear that little collective gasp in a team meeting and ignore it. You may choose to do nothing about it, but you will know what that sound means and you will know things you could do about it. You might be the only person in the room who knows what is happening, what it means, and has the ability to intervene in a meaningful way.

Are You Finished?

Of course not! The gift of Leadership INSIGHT marks a new beginning for most of you. If you have yet to actually work as a team leader, you have achieved a significant advantage over most potential leaders. You will be able to see more clearly from the beginning and, hopefully, avoid many mistakes.

For those of my readers with significant amounts of time as a leader, your journey is re-starting. You have had the benefit of many team situations that occurred in your past to use as validation points for the concepts that have been presented. Now that you have the benefit of Leadership INSIGHT, you will be able to re-visit the concepts that you previously learned to perform as a leader and test how valid they are. Some of those leadership behaviors will show themselves to have been tried and true. There will be some that you can choose to change.

You will be able to think about how you actually responded to team problems in the past and rethink them. How would you have acted if they had occurred after you had read this book? I would guess that your responses would be quite different.

Having a clear picture of what is happening as your team goes about its business, both at the surface and below, will make the need for evaluation and behavioral changes more evident. You will be better able to see the effects of different leadership interventions on your team and perform mid-course corrections. Now that you understand that interventions should be attempted based on the outcome you are trying to achieve, you will have more interventions from which to choose.

Leadership INSIGHT explains that the Law of Reinforcement works both ways: as a way to choose appropriate rewards for your subordinates, and in reverse as a way to understand why people behaved as they did. You know that the answer to the question "Why did he/they do that?" is always "Because he/they received a reward or avoided a punishment." Now you are better prepared to figure out the rest.

Leadership INSIGHT makes you aware of the process that underlies the discussions in you decision-making team. That opens an entire world of data that you may have never seen before. The more relevant data you have, the better will be your decisions.

You are more aware of the complexity of any situation where people are operating in a group. You can see them operating at multiple levels.

Leadership INSIGHT has made you more aware of how people talk about thoughts when they are really talking about their feelings. Knowing the difference helps you understand those people and deal with them more effectively.

With the concept of Locus of Control, you found a way to actually estimate the degree of control you and your subordinates think they have over events. That knowledge gives you an advantage in helping them make behavior improvements they want to make.

Leadership INSIGHT instills in you the understanding of the nature of work teams. Knowing what teams typically value and how they typically act gives you a set of signposts with which to recognize if and when your team is going off track.

In the discussion of guiding your team, Leadership INSIGHT introduced you to a set of tools with which you can move the team in more appropriate directions. You get a clearer picture of what they need to become more effective, a way to recognize when an intervention might be appropriate and a theory of which results your interventions should aim to achieve.

These Concepts Are Secret No More!

These are powerful tools. Like the tools in your garage or basement, the can be used for good or for harm. Use them thoughtfully and you needn't worry about using them poorly.

Chapter EIGHT
Afterthoughts

What happens now?

That's a good question. A lot depends on what you want. As I said in the first part of this book, Leadership INSIGHT is independent of the style of management you choose and the management philosophy in which you believe.

Most readers will not want to become professional team facilitators. They just want to be better at leading their teams. For those readers, I say, "Go forward unto your teams and do so with open eyes." You will be that much better as a leader because you will be more aware of what is actually happening in your team.

Will Leadership INSIGHT fix a "broken team"?

Leadership INSIGHT can't fix a broken team by itself, -- but it will help. The term "broken team" can have many possible meanings. In the example I cited where the Vice President of sales had long been planning to leave the team, nothing can immediately fix that team. The VP position needs to be filled and the team re-formed. If only one new person is added to that team, there will still need to be some repair work done. Unfortunately, that team felt betrayed by a team member. Learning to trust all of the reconstituted team members at a 100% level will take some time. There is, however, no question that it can be done successfully.

Most of the time, when a word like "broken" is applied to a team, it means that the team is not functioning well, even though all of the team members seem to be technically competent at their jobs. The team leader needs to reassess each member technically to be certain that they are all competent (hopefully with some extra potential). The leader, with or without professional help, needs to assess what developmental needs each member has and plan to help them get those needs fulfilled. Some team members may be working well within their total competency level and some may be barely on the edge of competency. The leader needs to know which case is relevant and take action to remedy the situation.

Assuming that the assessment tells the leader that the members are okay, the next thing to look at is "How are we functioning as a team? The process of doing this is simple in concept but somewhat difficult in practice.

In a nutshell, -- Picture a high-performance team and compare your team to that picture. How does my team differ in the way we do things from an ideal high-performance team? You can actually take a short test that will give you a rough approximation of the answer to that question. (See http://hrdusa.com/myteam.html) This article offers a short explanation of all the concepts, and provides a simple interpretation of your answers. Obviously, it then presents several alternatives to deal with the results.

Hiring a Professional to Assist

Although it is rarely possible, the best place to start building a championship team is from scratch. Each person can be assessed for both technical skills and compatibility with the other team members and with the corporate culture.

The more likely scenario is that such a team-building effort starts with the team leader thinking that the team could be performing at a higher level and wondering if anything could be done about it. The process of evaluating the team as a whole, each individual member and selecting a professional to assist you in building your team is thoroughly discussed in my book, "Grow

Your Team or Watch It Die!" It includes various tests and checklists to guide you in the process of making that decision and even a checklist for selecting and engaging a team-building professional. Most important, it also discusses psychological contracting within your team.

What if I want to learn more about becoming a Team Facilitator?

Team facilitation skills which go beyond the level described in this book are considered professional level skills. They require much practice and considerable commitment.

The skills are developed under the close supervision of heavily experienced facilitators. Everything is done on a one-to-one level. At the professional level, supervision takes the form of co-leading group sessions, followed by immediately discussing what went on during the session, focusing on each participant, where they are in their team development, and how to help them move in the right direction. The final part of that discussion is deciding what to do during the next team session and predicting what will happen in terms of the group's development and the development of each individual team member. Possible interventions are discussed and practiced.

Developing excellence in team facilitation skills has been one of the most rewarding accomplishments of my work life. I have found that being able to bring about changes in work team effectiveness is exceptionally satisfying and rewarding.

If you want more information see:

http://www.leadershipskillsusa.com/programs.html

How Does This Work?

Before we discuss going further in the area of advanced team leadership, let's spend a little time on the topic of the setting in which the learning takes place. Each environment has different effects.

The Learning Environment

Most of us have experienced the most common learning environment – the classroom. I use the term intending to include any environment in which there is a teacher who lectures (actively presents information) and students (people who passively absorb what is taught). It matters little whether this takes place in a school or university, a training room in a corporate setting, in a lecture hall or in the ballroom of a hotel with multiple rows of chairs facing a raised platform with a speakers' table.

The basic paradigm is the same -- an active presenter and a passive learner. The most extreme example of this paradigm is the online class. The active part is the computer screen presenting information and the passive part is the learner looking at the screen. This basic paradigm is acceptable if the learner's goal is only to input information (one way of saying "learning").

However, in learning skills, the rule is: "The more active the learner's participation, the better the learning." Skills are applied behavior.

My wife grew up in Queens, New York. I listened in amazement as she told me about her first set of tennis lessons. They took place in the instructor's apartment, which had 8-foot ceilings. She spent lesson after lesson swinging her tennis racket inside that apartment.

She explained that it was difficult and expensive to get court time in New York City. The indoor practice was the best they could do. In response, I explained that in Chicago, where I grew up, all the parks had free tennis courts which tended to be under-used. Lessons were free from park pros. Practice time was almost unlimited.

My wife eventually learned to play tennis. Those indoor sessions taught her some things about form, rules, etc. The real learnings took place when she got onto a real tennis court, and got the feel of the game. She got to see what she did well and what she needed to work on to improve her game.

It works similarly when learning how to lead others. You've got to do it to see the effects. What do you do that works well? What do you do that works moderately well? What do you do that fails completely? Which behaviors do you want to keep and which do you want to change?

If you want to change a behavior, how do you experiment? After all, you are at work. What you do counts. Is that the right place to try out new ways of doing things?

My answer is a resounding "NO!"

The Leadership Development Laboratory (LDL)

In the same way that a chemistry laboratory is a place to do experiments, with safety precautions and procedures in place, a leadership laboratory does the same thing (without the expensive equipment). The LDL can take place almost anywhere that a group can assemble. It is preferably off-site, quiet, without interruptions (read: NO cell phones or land lines) and calm.

It is a place where a group can interact. The members can assess whether or not their typical behaviors are working optimally and where they can experiment with new behaviors, if they choose to do so. The LDL has at its core the rule that experimentation is expected and appropriate and that the group will be supportive of behavioral experimentation.

Developing the LDL atmosphere usually takes a professional team facilitator and some time to establish. Theoretically, it could happen without professional help, but I have never seen or heard of a spontaneously developing LDL atmosphere.

Finally, the LDL is a solid platform from which preparation can be made to transfer the learnings to the workplace. This last part is critical, because that is the ultimate goal – more effective behavior in the work place. For more information on the topic of LDLs, see my booklet "Knowledge Isn't Power Until It Is Applied" on Amazon.com.

Team Leadership Skills Development

You've taken the first step – Learning about those aspects of what happens in a group that most people don't even see. Let's look at what is done in a Leadership Skills Development environment. There are basically four steps to the process:

The individuals learn how they see themselves.

Self-assessment is almost always the initial part of the process. It is difficult to change behavior without having a clear picture of how you see that behavior when working with the group.

The individuals learn how others see them in the group setting.

Learning how others in the group see you is a very difficult, but vitally necessary step in learning to lead. The difference between how you see yourself and how you come across to others is the degree to which you don't perceive reality optimally and also is an indication of how much and where changes in behavior may be necessary.

Assess the effectiveness of current leadership behaviors?

The individual learns how effective her current behaviors are in leading the group (or, for that matter, in being an effective follower). The individual uses this information to decide whether or not a behavior change is desired. It is in this area where experimentation takes place. If the new behavior works, keep it – if not, try something else.

Learning to make the changes permanent in the work place.

Finally, the individual makes plans to transfer the new

behaviors to the workplace. More importantly, the team commits to support each of its members in their attempts to change their behavior in the work world.

Making permanent changes in a person's behavior is not a simple process. It takes time and support. For more information on the topic see:

http://www.leadershipskillsusa.com/leadership.html

I would greatly appreciate Feedback on this book.

Since I have never seen this material ever presented in book form before, I would be grateful if you would send me your comments and/or questions on this topic.

Have I left anything out?

Should I go into greater depth on one or more topics in the book?

How can I help you to become a better leader?

How can I help your work team or organization become more effective?

Send comments or questions to:

drrosner@hrdusa.com

Review Request

If you enjoyed this book and found it useful, I'd be very grateful if you'd post an honest review. Your support really does matter and it really does make a difference. I do read all the reviews so I can get your feedback and I do make changes as a result of that feedback.

If you'd like to leave a review then all you need to do is go to the review section on the book's Amazon page. You'll see a big button that says "Write a customer review" – click that and you're good to go!

Thanks for your support.

Yours in friendship,

References:

Cohen A.M. & Smith, R.D, The Critical Incident in Growth Groups: Theory and Technique, University Associates, 1976

Rotter, J. B. (1954). Social learning and clinical psychology. New York: Prentice-Hall.

Rotter, J.B. (1966) Generalized expectancies for internal versus external control of reinforcement, Psychological Monographs, 80, (1, Whole No. 609).

Sherif, M., Harvey, O.J., White, B.J., Hood, W. & Sherif, C.W. (1961). *Intergroup conflict and cooperation: The robbers cave experiment.* Norman, OK: The University Book Exchange.

ABOUT THE AUTHOR

Dr. Phillip E. Rosner

In 1972, Dr. Rosner completed his doctorate in a new field, Organizational Psychology. He was the first such graduate in the history of the university. Virtually every phase of the program had to be created either by him or for him. .

In 1976, Dr. Rosner had just finished a four year stint as a Corporate Psychologist for a large international consulting firm. Those years allowed him to work with the CEOs of several Fortune 100 companies and get involved in complex organizational interventions that gave him practical experience available to few.

In that year Human Resource Development, Inc. was founded. (The name refers to "the human resource" of a company -- it's people.) During the subsequent years, Dr. Rosner has trained several Organizational Psychologists and worked for a wide variety of companies in many industries. He continues to serve as Trusted Advisor to a number of "old" and new clients.

He lives in Marietta, GA with his wife, Peri. He has two grown children, Alicia who lives and works in Austin, TX and Seth, who lives in Columbia, MO with his son, Jacob and his wife, Chelsea Garneau-Rosner, PhD, who is an Assistant Professor at the University of Missouri.

www.ingramcontent.com/pod-product-compliance
Lightning Source LLC
Chambersburg PA
CBHW031301090426